Mor a Dickens MBE** was born in 1915, and was the grea granddaughter of Charles Dickens. Expelled from St Paul Girls' School, she was then sent to a finishing scho in France, before returning home to life as a debutante The deb scene and the dances were absolute agony. ' look at the waiters and the maids at balls and ¢ certain that they were having a better time than ;o I wanted to belong with them, down there here was a bit of life.' And indeed, she then spent irs as a cook and general servant. She later wrote au er experiences in her first book, *One Pair of Hands* (193 , which made her a bestseller at the age of twenty-two d immediately established her reputation as a write In her career she wrote over fifty books, including the *llyfoot* novels, and for twenty years wrote a much-lo column for *Woman's Own*. She was also involved he NSPCC, the RSPCA and the Samaritans. She 1992, and is survived by two daughters.

One Pair of Hands

Monica Dickens

EBURY
PRESS

1 3 5 7 9 10 8 6 4 2

Published in 2011 by Ebury Press, an imprint of Ebury Publishing
A Random House Group company
First published by Michael Joseph in 1939

The Random House Group Limited Reg. No. 954009

Addresses for companies within the Random House Group can be
found at www.randomhouse.co.uk

A CIP catalogue record for this book is available from
the British Library

The Random House Group Limited supports The Forest Stewardship Council
(FSC®), the leading international forest certification organisation. Our books
carrying the FSC label are printed on FSC® certified paper. FSC is the only
forest certification scheme endorsed by the leading environmental organisations,
including Greenpeace. Our paper procurement policy can be found at
www.randomhouse.co.uk/environment

MIX
Paper from
responsible sources
FSC® C016897

Printed in the UK by CPI Cox & Wyman, Reading, RG1 8EX

ISBN 9780091944681

To buy books by your favourite authors and register for offers visit
www.randomhouse.co.uk

Chapter One

I was fed up. As I lay awake in the grey small hours of an autumn morning, I reviewed my life. Three a.m. is not the most propitious time for meditation, as everyone knows, and a deep depression was settling over me.

I had just returned from New York, where the crazy cyclone of gaiety in which people seem to survive over there had caught me up, whirled me blissfully round, and dropped me into a London which seemed flat and dull. I felt restless, dissatisfied, and abominably bad-tempered.

'Surely,' I thought, 'there's something more to life than just going out to parties that one doesn't enjoy, with people one doesn't even like? What a pointless existence it is – drifting about in the hope that something may happen to relieve the monotony. Something has got to be done to get me out of this rut.'

In a flash it came to me:

'I'll have a job!'

I said it out loud and it sounded pretty good to me, though my dog didn't seem to be deeply moved. The more I thought about it, the better I liked the idea, especially from the point of view of making some money.

My mind sped away for a moment, after the fashion of all minds in bed, and showed me visions of big money – furs – a new car – but I brought it back to earth with an effort to wonder for what sort of a job I could possibly qualify. I reviewed the possibilities.

Since leaving school I had trained rather half-heartedly for various things. I had an idea, as everyone does at that age, that I should be a roaring success on the stage. When I came back from being 'finished' in Paris, I had begged to be allowed to have dramatic training.

'Try anything once,' said my parents, so off I went, full of hope and ambition, to a London dramatic school. I hadn't been there more than two weeks before I and everybody else in the place discovered that I couldn't act, and, probably, never would be able to. This was discouraging, but I ploughed on, getting a greater inferiority complex every day. Part of the policy of this school is to 'knock the corners off the girls' (not the men, they are too rare and precious). It is only the tough, really ambitious girls who weather the storm of biting sarcasm and offensive personal remarks that fall on their cowed heads. This is a good thing, really, as it means that only the ones with real talent and endurance go through with it to that even tougher life ahead. The uncertain and inept ones like myself are discouraged at the start from a career in which they could never make a success, and so are saved many heartbreaks later on.

Once having made up my mind that I had no vocation, I enjoyed my year there immensely, and walked about the stage quite happily as the maid, or somebody's sister, with hands and feet growing larger every minute. Gazing into a still pool at sunset, or registering grief, fear, and ecstasy in rapid succession, was wonderful fun, too: especially when performed in the company of fifty other girls in rather indecent black tights.

It didn't occur to me that it might be a little irritating for the authorities to have someone trailing unambitiously about in the dust raised by the star pupils. No one was more surprised than myself, therefore, when I found myself – thrown out, figuratively speaking, on my ear – standing on the pavement with my books under one arm and my black tights under the other.

The next possibility was dressmaking. I dismissed that, too, at once, because it has always seemed to me to be the resort of inefficient, but certainly decorative, society girls, who are given jobs in dress shops, in the hope that they will introduce their rich friends. After that, they stand about the place in streamlined attitudes, wearing marvellous clothes and expressions of suffering superiority.

That didn't seem quite my style, so I turned to cooking. That was the thing which interested me most and about which I thought I knew quite a lot. I had had a few lessons from my 'Madame' in Paris, but my real interest was aroused by lessons I had at a wonderful school of French cookery in London.

I went there quite unable to boil so much as an egg and came out with Homard Thermidor and Crêpes Suzette at my fingertips. I was still unable to boil an egg, however, or roast a joint of beef. The simple things weren't considered worth teaching, so I had a short spell at a very drab school of English cooking, where there were a great many pupils clamouring for the attention of the two ancient spinsters who taught us. When they hadn't time to tell me what to cook next, it was: 'Get washed up, Miss Dickens,' and Miss Dickens had to clean up other people's messes at the sink, till, at last, if she was lucky she was allowed to make a rock-cake.

When I told my family that I was thinking of taking a cooking job, the roars of laughter were rather discouraging. No one believed that I could cook at all, as I had never had a chance to practise at home. Our cook, aged sixty-five and slightly touched, had ruled in the kitchen for thirty years and had an irritating tendency to regard the saucepans, stove, and indeed all the kitchen fittings as her own property.

I once crept down there when I thought she was asleep in her room to try out an omelette. Noiselessly I removed a frying-pan from its hook and the eggs from their cupboard. It was the pop of the gas that woke her, I think, for I was just breaking the first egg when a pair of slippered feet shuffled round the door and a shriek of horror caused me to break the egg on the floor. This disaster, together with the fact that I was using her one very special beloved and delicately nurtured frying-pan, upset cook so much that she locked herself in the larder with all the food and we had to make our Sunday dinner off bananas.

If the family weren't going to be helpful I would look for a job all by myself and not tell them about it till I'd got one. I had no idea of exactly what job I should apply for, so I decided to go to an agency. I had seen one advertised in a local paper, so as soon as there was no one about to say, 'Where are you going?' I clapped on my mildest hat, and rushed out of the house in search of it. I was wildly excited, and as nervous as if I were going to a stage audition. Finding the place quite easily, I tore up three flights of stairs, and swung breathlessly through a door which said, 'Enter without knocking, if you please.'

The dingy, bottle-green atmosphere of the office sobered me, and I sat meekly down on the edge of a chair and could see my nose shining out of the corner of my eye. I thought perhaps it was a good thing, it might look more earnest. The woman at the desk opposite scrutinized me for a while through rimless pince-nez, and I became absorbed in the question of whether or not she wore a wig. I had just decided that it was too undesirably shabby to be anything but her own hair, when I realized that she was murmuring questions at me. I answered in a hoarse whisper because it seemed to be the thing, and because all of a sudden I started to feel rather pathetic. She hinted in a delicate way that she wondered why I was looking for this sort of job, so I felt impelled to give her a glimpse of a widowed mother and a desperate struggle against poverty. I almost made myself believe in the pathos of it, and we had to cough and change the subject. I felt even more pathetic when she told me that it would be difficult to get a job without experience or references. She rustled about among her papers for a bit and I wondered whether I ought to leave, when the telephone on her desk rang. While she was conducting a cryptic conversation she kept looking at me. Then I heard her say:

'As a matter of fact, I've got someone in the office at this very moment who might suit.' She wrote down a number, and my spirits soared as I took the slip of paper she held out to me, saying: 'Ring up this lady. She wants a cook immediately. In fact, you would have to start tomorrow by cooking a dinner for ten people. Could you manage that, I wonder?'

'Oh, yes,' said I – never having cooked for more than four in my life. I thanked her profusely, paid a shilling, and dashed out to the nearest telephone box. I collected my wits, powdered my nose, took a deep breath, and dialled the number. A piping voice at the other end informed me that I was speaking to Miss Cattermole. I assured her, with all the bluff at my command, that I was just what she was looking for.

'Are you sure?' she kept saying. 'Are you *sure*? It's a celebration for my brother – just home from B.A., you know.' I expressed suitable awe, though for all I knew B.A. might have been anything from an outpost of Empire to a long spell of Penal Servitude, and she decided to engage me for the dinner-party, anyway, and as a permanency if I fulfilled the promise of my self-praise. I asked her what tomorrow's menu was to be.

'Just a small, simple dinner: lobster cocktails, soup, turbot Mornay, pheasants with vegetables, fruit salad, and a savoury.' In rather a shaken voice, I promised to turn up in good time, and rang off.

I spent the intervening hours feverishly reading cookery books, and wishing that I hadn't let myself in for something about which I knew so little. My family were still highly amused at the idea of my attempting it, which didn't increase my confidence. I told my mother she was a widow and she took it quite well.

Miss Cattermole lived in Dulwich in one of the most depressing houses ever seen. It had a great many grimy turrets and smatterings of stained glass, and though quite small, was approached by a semi-circular drive round an unhealthy tangle of laurels. I rang at the back door and the depression of the house closed round me as I was admitted by a weary-looking maid. She was so thin that her dress and apron drooped on her, and even her cap fell over her eyes as if the whole lot wanted to slide despairingly to the ground. I followed her through a sort of stone rabbit-warren to where an ancient brooding figure sat hunched in a chair in the sitting-room. She was introduced to me on a note of reverent horror, as: 'Nannie' – evidently a family pensioner who had transferred her awesome sway from the nursery to the basement. It was quite obvious why Miss Cattermole had difficulty in keeping a cook. The maid was called away by a bell and Nannie condescended to show me the kitchen, though I could see that she hated me at sight.

As I started to prepare the dinner I began to share her gloomy view of myself, as it dawned on me more and more that high-class cooking lessons are all very well, but a little practical experience is necessary, too, in order to cope with the vicissitudes that crop up in the kitchen.

I made the fruit salad first. That was quite easy, as all I had to do was cut up fruit and mess it together in a bowl. After a bit, I got tired of scraping the pith off oranges, and I also caught sight of the time, so I pushed the rest, all stringy, to the bottom of the dish, and rushed the pheasants into the oven. Then I washed the vegetables sketchily, and put them on to cook. Feverishly I opened the tins of lobster. When I came to from the agonized delirium of a torn thumb, I was confronted by the problem of how on earth one made a lobster cocktail. I started to make them into a sticky mess with some tomato, thinned down with a little of my life-blood. At this critical point the mistress of the house careered into the kitchen in full feather.

The first impression one got of Miss Cattermole was like looking into one of those kaleidoscopes, in which coloured beads whirl about in a dazzle of changing patterns. When your eyes got used to her, she resolved into a mass of multi-coloured scarves, sewn haphazardly together, so that loose ends waved gaily from unlikely places to the answering flutter of straggling orange-wool hair. Out of this profusion, a pair of beady eyes darted a piercing glance of horror at my poor lobster.

'Oh, dear!' she shrilled. 'Is that the way you make lobster cocktails? It looks funny to me; oh, dear, I do hope everything's going to be all right. Are you *sure* –' I saw the eyes jump round to where the turbot lay keeping warm. I had cooked it too early and it was getting harder and drier every minute while it waited for its sauce to cover it.

There was a desperate sinking feeling inside me, and I had to call to my aid all the bluff I knew.

I threw a careless shake of red pepper over the prawns, and, with the air of one who knows so much that it's almost boring, I drawled:

'Well, actually, I was talking to a famous chef the other

day, and he gave me a special recipe – they use it at the Savoy, too. I thought you might like to have it, but, of course, if you prefer the ordinary –' I shrugged my shoulders, watching her closely from under scornfully-drooped eyelids. Would she buy it? She did. I had luckily hit upon a good line, for that gaudy exterior cloaked a drab little snobbish soul. She retired under my supercilious gaze and I returned frantically to my lobster. Dinner was at eight and it was already a quarter past seven. I discovered some cream and poured that on; the lobster began to look more appetizing; I wanted more cream and there was none, but I discovered three milk bottles in the larder, so I opened them all and used the top part. The lobster looked all right now, so I started to put them into their sherry glasses. I broke one, of course, and had to creep into the pantry when the sad thin maid wasn't looking to find another. I rushed back to the kitchen to sweep up the broken bits, as I could see a pair of silver slippers descending the stairs. I only just had time to kick the glass under the stove and pour more water on to the potatoes, which had boiled dry and were starting to burn, before taking up my stance, negligently stirring the soup. She smelled the potatoes, of course, so I opened the oven door and took her mind off them with a fine smell of roasting as I basted the pheasants.

'It just came into my mind that some tomatoes and mushrooms would be rather tasty lying round the dish,' she said; 'there should be some in the larder.' My silent curses followed her as she withdrew. I would never be ready in time! I put the tomatoes into the soup to loosen their skins and one of them burst and I had to strain the soup. Thank goodness I had been taught at the French school that mushrooms taste better unpeeled. I put them on to cook, and the next ten minutes were a mad turmoil as everything decided to finish cooking itself at once. I rushed about, snatching things away here and there as they were about to burn. I turned the oven down, and put everything inside to keep warm, and stood back wiping the sweat off my brow and feeling rather pleased with myself. Even the savoury was ready – it would be pretty dried up by the time it appeared, but it was a load off my mind.

I only just got this done before the hired waitresses came in with trays and said that the guests were there and they wanted to serve dinner. I got it away all right as far as the fish, forgetting to put the sherry in the soup, but I was past bothering about trifles like that. I was carefully carving the pheasants, calculating that it would take them a little time to drink their soup and toy with their fish while conversing elegantly of this and that. However, they evidently had nothing to say to each other and were concentrating on quick eating, because the waitresses came back for the pheasants long before they were ready. In a frenzy, I tore the wretched birds limb from limb with my bare hands, and scattered mushrooms over the ragged pieces as best I could. Nannie had arrived in the kitchen at this point and was observing my distress with the utmost satisfaction. She kept either sniffing or clicking her teeth, whichever it was it was maddening, and I said:

'Would you mind taking the vegetables out of the oven?'

She shuffled off to get a cloth, and took care not to return till I'd done it myself. Black despair settled on me and I could have cried with exhaustion and hatred of everybody in this horrible house. I remembered to make the coffee. Luckily Nannie didn't see it boil up all over the stove. Things were a little calmer now, except that dirty dishes kept on arriving in astonishing numbers and being piled up wherever there was an inch of space. The sad maid – her name was Addie I discovered – and the two waitresses were behaving like people acting in a play. They would sweep into the kitchen as if coming off the stage into the wings, with trays held high and a tense expression of hauteur still on their faces, relax for a moment in the frenzy of getting the new dishes loaded, and glide off again with faces prepared to make their next entrance. The nurse and I were left like stage hands among the debris, as if having seen a glimpse of another world; we almost listened for the applause of the unseen audience.

The washing up took an age. I began to regret the days when a huge dish was put on the middle of the table and everyone helped themselves with their fingers. It was finished at last, and we all sat down in the sitting-room round the unappetizing remains of the feast, 'hotted up' by me. I was too tired to do more than drink a cup of tea. They regarded me with pity, and Nannie said, 'Slimmin', I suppose – mad I call it,' as she packed potato away behind her well-filled black alpaca. Addie ate rapaciously and I wondered at her thinness. I was enlightened, however, when her apology for passing her plate for a third helping was: 'It's me little strangers, there's no satisfyin' 'em, it seems.'

This led to other interesting topics. Nannie's feet, it appeared, were inclined to 'draw' in the damp, and Violet, one of the waitresses, had some information on the subject of varicose veins. The other waitress, whose name sounded like Mrs Haddock, had a daughter who had just had a bad time with her first, so, not to be outdone, I told them about my dropped arches. This went down well, and I went up a bit in their estimation. Cigarettes were lit, and we settled down to a cosy discussion of the people upstairs.

'Some people,' said Addie in her rather moaning voice, 'have got a nerve. That Mrs Bewmont, I mean to say, asked for a second sponge finger, straight she did. "Well," I said to myself, "what cheek, eh?"'

'Well I never. *She* never took one.'

'Didn't she then? Too busy talking to his Lordship, I dessay. "Go it, my lady," I says to myself, "we seen you without your party manners."'

'What about Miss May? She got married, didn't she? Isn't she going to have a baby yet?'

'No, dear – she can't, I've heard. It's 'is fault, they say, but of course –'

I was beginning to feel a trifle uncomfortable, and was relieved when, at this point, the drawing-room bell broke into Addie's revelations.

'Oh, bells, bells, bells, they'd drive you mad,' said Violet calmly as she rose without haste to answer the summons. I thought it was about time I was going, so I went and put my coat on. I wanted to know what time I had to come the next day, and nothing had as yet been settled about my wages.

Violet came downstairs again and said: '*She* wants to see you before you go.'

'She' was in the hall, her plumage drooping a little from the strain of sociability. 'Ah, Miss Dickens!' I could see she was trying to carry something off, as her voice was higher than ever, and falsely bright. 'I really don't think I can settle anything permanent just now, so please don't bother to come tomorrow. Thank you *so* much. *Good* night!' She pressed some coins into my hand and vanished into the drawing-room. When the door had shut behind her on the well of voices, I opened my hand on two half-crowns and a shilling.

'Well,' I said to myself, as I banged out into the Dulwich night and nearly fell into the laurels, 'what a cheek, eh?'

Chapter Two

I think Miss Cattermole must have refrained from telling the agency what she thought of me, for they rang me up a few days later and offered me another job. This time it was a Mrs Robertson, who wanted someone twice a week to do washing and ironing and odd jobs. As I had already assured the agency that I was thoroughly domesticated in every way, I didn't feel like admitting that I was the world's worst ironer.

They gave me the address, and I went along there in a clean starched apron which I hoped made me look crisp and efficient. The porter of the flats let me in, as Mrs Robertson was out, but she had left a note for me, and a pile of washing on the bathroom floor. I sorted it out, and it was not attractive. It consisted mainly of several grubby and rather ragged pairs of corsets and a great many small pairs of men's socks and stockings in a horrid condition of stickiness.

I made a huge bowl of soapsuds, and dropped the more nauseating articles in with my eyes shut. I washed and rinsed and squeezed for about an hour and a half.

There was no one but me to answer the telephone, which always rang when I was covered in soap to the elbow. I accepted a bridge party for the owner of the corsets, and a day's golfing for the wearer of the socks, but did not feel in a position to give an opinion on the state of cousin Mary's health.

I had just finished hanging out the clothes, and had wandered into the drawing-room to see what sort of books they had, when I heard a latch key in the door. I flew back to the bathroom, and was discovered diligently tweaking out the fingers of gloves when Mrs Robertson walked in. It had occurred to me that she must be a very trusting person to allow a complete stranger the run of her flat, and I now realized that it was probably because she was the soul of honesty herself, that she expected everyone else to be the same. Her large blue eyes gazed candidly on the world, from a face that shone with integrity. She gave me a hearty smile and a handshake, and looked round to inspect my labours. If she expected everyone to be honest, she also expected them to be as efficient as herself. She was horrified to see that I had not hung the stockings up by the heels, and told me so with a charming frankness. However, she still wanted me to come back the next day to iron the things I had washed, so my heart warmed towards her, and I offered to make her a cup of tea. Mr Robertson arrived just as I was going out, and we collided at the front door. He threw me a terrific glance upwards, for he was a fiery man, and scuttled for safety into his dressing-room.

I returned the next day, still crisp and efficient, and scorched Mrs Robertson's best *crêpe de Chine* camisole. She was more than frank in her annoyance over this trifling mishap and it made me nervous. The climax came when I dropped the electric iron on the floor and it gave off a terrific burst of blue sparks. I supposed it had fused, and Mrs Robertson came hurrying in at the sound of the crash, and she knew it had. It was all very awkward, and I felt very small indeed under her candid remarks. It ended by her paying me at the rate of a shilling an hour for the time I had put in, and a tacit agreement being formed between us that I should never appear again. I just caught a glimpse of Mr Robertson flitting into a doorway as I came into the hall. I was sorry not to have known him better, we could have been friends, I think – except for the sticky socks.

Well, so far I didn't seem to have been much of a success as a working girl. I wasn't exactly piling up money in large quantities either, and the rate of pay didn't come anywhere near compensating for the mental agonies that I had undergone. I was still undaunted, however, and told myself that there are so many people in the world that it doesn't matter if one doesn't hit it off with one or two of them. I pinned my faith in the whispering woman in the agency, and went and had a heart-to-heart talk with her.

'What I want is something where I'll really get a chance to get some practical experience,' I told her.

'Well, we have one or two people asking for cook-generals,' she said. 'You might go and see this Miss Faulkener, at Chelsea. She wants someone to do the work of a very small flat, and cook dinner at night, and sometimes lunch. You ought to be able to manage that, I think.' She gazed at me thoughtfully, but without much confidence. 'Well, anyway, there's no harm in having an interview. Here's the address.'

I rang up Miss Faulkener, and she told me to come and see her that afternoon. The burning question of what to wear exercised me very much. Should I dress the part in two slashing shades of green and Woolworth ear-rings?

No, I would keep up the pretence of tragic gentility – plain, but clean and honest. A black coat and an uncompromising black felt hat would meet the case. Mourning, perhaps, for 'the Dad'. I might be a soldier's daughter, and he had told me with his last breath to 'Take care of your mother, the gallant little woman.'

I added a pair of cotton gloves to the outfit and went off, full of hope and very excited, to Miss Faulkener's flat off the King's Road. A sharp-featured maid opened the door and looked me over suspiciously.

'You come after the job?'

'Yes,' I whispered humbly.

'Got an appointment?'

'Yes.' I gave her my name, and she let me in reluctantly. I stood shifting my feet in the narrow hall, while she disappeared through a door, presumably to give a report on me to someone inside. Eventually she came out and told me I could go in. I found myself in one of those long rooms that have an archway in the middle and velvet curtains to divide it into drawing-room and dining-room. I was in the drawing-room end. On a sofa in front of a coal fire, groomed to the last eyebrow, sat my prospective employer. Though quite young, she had a self-confident poise beyond her years. Undeniably attractive, there was yet a hard, almost inhuman quality about the faultlessness of her appearance. She didn't look the sort of girl who could be persuaded to buy a dud article like myself, unless she wanted to of her own free will.

She told me to sit down, and scrutinized me pretty closely while we talked. It was a funny feeling to think that I was in her power to be accepted or rejected with contumely, and I had a strong schoolgirl desire to giggle.

'What experience have you had, and have you references?' I knew this was bound to come, but nevertheless it was still a disturbing question. I had thought of an answer, though, and got it out fast, stumbling a little in my desire to appear eager and worthy.

'Well, you see, I haven't actually had a job quite like

this before, but I've kept house for my mother for quite a time, and also, I've done quite a lot of cooking for dinner parties at various houses.' (Oh, Miss Cattermole, how art thou magnified!)

Then I gave her exaggerated accounts of my training in cookery, and sat back to let her think it over.

'Well, yes,' she said thoughtfully, 'I must say I'd rather you had more actual experience, but I'm in a hurry to get someone as my Mrs Baker, who let you in, wants to go tomorrow. Her father's ill. I don't want to be left without anybody. You really think you could manage the work all right?'

Trying to hit on a nice mixture of pride and deprecation, I assured her that I could. I hadn't the slightest idea how much money I ought to ask for.

She said: 'How about twenty-five shillings a week? Sunday afternoon and evening off, and one half-day a week.'

It sounded quite a lot to me, for something that I thought I was rather going to enjoy. She looked an amusing woman, and it would be marvellous to have the run of a kitchen to mess in to my heart's content. It was all fixed up; I was to start the next day. It seemed too good to be true to think that I'd really landed the job. In my enthusiasm, even the idea of getting up early seemed quite rosy. I asked her what time I had to be there in the mornings.

'I have my breakfast in bed at a quarter past nine, so if

you get here in time to get that ready, and lay this fire, that'll be all right. You can get this room done after that, as I don't get up very early.'

I could picture her, lying in bed, holding long telephone conversations, wearing something rather pink and lacy. I was sure she had lovely night-dresses.

She indicated that the interview was at an end, and told me to go and find Mrs Baker, who would show me where everything was. I found her in the kitchen. She was much pleasanter now that I was an accepted member of the household and not a suspicious intruder, and quite unburdened her soul to me over a pot of strong black tea. I heard all about her father's illness. The details were terrifying; it seemed to me about time someone went and looked after him.

'It's a long time now since I lived at 'ome,' she said. 'Dad and Mr Baker, they never could get on together, so we went out Streatham way and set up on our own. Then when Mr B was called above, with pneumonia, poor soul, six years ago, that was, I went into service. Been with Miss Faulkener nearly a year now. Ever such a nice young lady she is, but particular. Oh, my, yes. Some folks seem to 'ave nothin' better to do all day than to run their fingers along the shelves, lookin' for dirt. Not that I'd say anything against her, mind, she's always been very nice to me, I'm sure. Her parents are divorced. I expect you won't mind that.'

She said this last with such emphasis, and looked at me so severely that it was obvious that she didn't approve herself and would be shocked but not surprised if I did.

I said airily: 'Ah well, of course, Mrs Baker, in these days, you know, one has to make allowances; after all, it's happening every day.'

'Those whom God hath joined together –' she replied sternly. That's the one remark to which there is never any answer, so I suggested that she might show me round a bit. It was a dear little kitchen and beautifully clean. I looked forward to having it to myself, though I was afraid it wouldn't look quite so spotless after I'd been in occupation for a bit.

The flat consisted of Miss Faulkener's bedroom, a tasteful chamber of the peach satin and white woolly rug order, a spare room, bathroom, and the drawing-cum-dining-room which I had already seen. There didn't look a great lot to do – not that I'd had any experience of housework, but Mrs Baker took care to point out that all the floors were parquet.

'You'd be surprised at the amount of polishing they take.'

I pursed my lips knowingly and nodded, trying to look as though I'd been polishing floors all my life.

She then told me a lot of things about the routine of the establishment. I didn't take in all of them, but I was pleased to hear that Miss Faulkener took an interest in food and 'liked things done appetizing'. It would give me plenty of scope for practising.

I suddenly remembered that I must go and buy a uniform before the shops shut, so Mrs Baker and I went out of each other's life and I made tracks for an Oxford Street store where I could get something on my mother's account.

They had a huge variety of really quite decorative uniforms. 'There's no need to look drab even if I am only a general,' I thought to myself. I bought a plain blue dress and some very tricky little frilled aprons with cuffs and collars to match. I tried on a few caps, but decided I looked too like a waitress, and anyway it was rather the modern idea for maids to revolt against wearing caps. I finished off my trousseau by getting some bright-coloured overalls to ward off depression in the early morning and a very attractive peasant apron for cooking.

I rushed home to try on my uniform, and was so fascinated by it that I had to keep it on the entire evening. I was to get sick of the sight of it only too soon, when it began to wilt a little under the stress of work!

I went to bed early, with the cook's alarm clock at my side, but in spite of that I didn't sleep well. I kept dozing off and then waking with a start, thinking that the alarm had gone wrong and I had overslept. Its strident note eventually broke into a confused dream about floor polishing and terrified me right out of bed into the damp chill of a November morning. I rigged myself out in my uniform, which was cold with the unfriendliness of all new garments, and only put on just enough make-up to establish my self-respect. My breakfast arrived at this point, and I bolted down some coffee and rushed off, clutching my overalls and aprons, feeling distinctly queasy about the stomach, and, arriving in good time, let myself in, feeling like an old hand. I had a look over her letters, but there was nothing that looked exciting, so I took myself off to the kitchen. It was looking rather inhumanly neat, and was distinctly cold. There was no boiler as it was a flat, and a small refrigerator stood in one corner. I hung my coat behind the door, put on an overall, and, rolling up my sleeves, prepared to attack the drawing-room fire. I found the wood and coal, but I couldn't see what Mrs Baker had used to collect the ash in. However, I found a wooden box which I thought would do, and took the coal along the passage in that. I hadn't laid a fire since my girl-guide days, but it seemed quite simple, and I took the ashes out to the dustbin, leaving a little trail of cinders behind me from a broken corner of the box. The trouble about housework is that whatever you do seems to lead to another job to do or a mess to clear up. I put my hand against the wall while I was bending down to sweep up the cinders and made a huge grubby mark on the beautiful cream-coloured paint. I rubbed at it gingerly with a soapy cloth and the dirt came off all right, but an even larger stain remained, paler than the rest of the paint, and with a hard, grimy outline. I didn't dare wash it any more, and debated moving the grandfather clock over to hide it. However, it was now a quarter past nine, so I had to leave it to its fate and pray that Miss Faulkener wouldn't notice, as it was time to get her breakfast ready. She only wanted coffee and toast and grapefruit, which didn't take long. I tried to make some butter balls, but though I rotated the pats in the approved style something was wrong somewhere, because the butter just stuck to them in a shapeless mess. I had to give it up as it was half past nine, so I combed my hair and powdered my nose in an effort to look like 'the fresh-faced maid', who draws people's curtains in novels, 'letting in the full radiance of the morning sun'. I needn't have bothered, for she was buried under the peach eiderdown and remained there while I put down the tray and drew the curtains on the beginnings of a fog. I turned on the gas-fire and wondered whether I ought to wake her up, so I coughed. The eiderdown heaved and I went out.

I had dusted the living-room, swept all the dirt down the passage and into the kitchen, and gone through the usual tedious business of chasing it about, trying to get it into the dustpan before her bell and back-door bell rang at the same moment. People don't realize when they put their finger on a button what a chaotic effect it has on the maid's nerves. I stood quivering in the middle of the kitchen, recovering from the shock while I tried to decide which to answer first. The back door was the nearest, so I opened it on a man in a bowler hat and bicycling clips who tapped a paper pad and said 'Grosher.'

'Do you mean orders?'

'Yesh, mish.'

'Well, I don't really know yet –'

'O.K., Mish, I'll do the other flats firsht and call back.'

'All right.'

He went on up the outside stairs whistling, and I rushed to the bedroom, wiping my hands on my overall before going in.

'Good morning, Monica, I hope you're getting on all right.'

Just as I thought, very expensive-looking pink satin and lace –

'Yes, thank you – madam.' I'd been practising this at home, but it still sounded a little self-conscious. After much deliberation I'd chosen it in preference to ma'am or 'm, or even *madarm,* which is popular in some basement circles.

'I just want to talk about food. Have you got a pencil and paper?' I went back to the kitchen for it, and there was the milkman jangling outside the door. I had to rush back to the bedroom, ask 'How much milk?' rush back to the kitchen, receive a bottle, look for the little book to check it in, and then rush back to the bedroom to take up the threads. By the time I'd got there a man wanted to be let in to read the meter.

This incessant conflict between the summonses of upper and lower regions is one of the most annoying things about domestic service. One gets used to it in time, but it is always a bit of a strain on the nerves.

Eventually we got down to the food question. 'I shall be out to lunch,' she said, 'but there's a gentleman coming to dinner. Perhaps you could suggest something nice?' All cooks' minds are a hopeless blank when confronted with this question, and mine was no exception. She laughed, realizing this, and I liked her. She looked very gay when she laughed, and much more friendly.

I daringly suggested a mushroom *soufflé* to start with. It was a bit of a risk as I'd only made one once at the cookery school, but she was delighted. Evidently Mrs Baker's cooking hadn't run to much more than plain things, which was a help, as it meant less chance of unfavourable comparison between us. We fixed the other courses, and I rushed back to the kitchen as I could hear that the 'Grosher' was back again. I polished him off, and after that dealt in rapid succession with various butchers, fishmongers, greengrocers, etc., not to mention a small boy with a huge hat-box. A few original and pungent remarks about the weather had to be exchanged with each.

I'd never realized what a sociable lot of back-door traffic there is, especially in a house where the mistress doesn't order the things at the shops herself. It adds a great deal of amusement to life, but it is a little harrying when one is trying to do thousands of other things at the same time.

The telephone rang while Miss Faulkener was in the bath, so I had to go into the bedroom and answer it. When I picked it up and said, 'Hullo!' a voice at the other end surprised me with:

'Good morning, darling sweet.'

'This is Miss Faulkener's maid,' I said reprovingly.

'Oh, Lord! That's not Mrs Baker, surely?'

'No sir, Mrs Baker left and I have taken her place.'

'Well, I hope your cooking's as nice as your voice.'

'I beg your pardon?' I thought him a trifle impertinent, but I must remember my place.

'Well, it couldn't be worse than Mrs B's.'

At this point my mistress drifted in from the bathroom in a cloud of perfume and a pink satin dressing-gown, and wondered what I was conversing about.

'Someone for me?'

'Yes, madam. Here is Miss Faulkener to speak to you now, sir.'

I put down the receiver, and went out of the room as she picked it up with a 'Really, darling, must you always ring up when I'm in the bath?'

Her 'best boy' evidently, as we say below stairs. I wondered if it was he who was coming to dinner.

I had to do the bathroom now, and was delighted to see that she was not one of those people who leave the place in a sickening mess – with cigarette ends and hairs all over everything.

She had lots of scented things to put in the bath, and I approved of her toothpaste. Her sponge was not greasy and sticky from long use, and I liked her even more – I crashed around among the bottles and things with a cloth and wiped the bath.

I kept my eyes severely turned away from one piece of furniture lest it should remind me that it was my duty to clean it or something. I struck at that.

Miss Faulkener went out soon, looking smart in black, with a lovely fur coat, so I made her bed, and spent an intriguing ten minutes among her personal effects. The Voice on the Telephone stood on the dressing-table seen from two aspects, in one of those double-folding frames. I studied him carefully and found him rather attractive in a military-looking way, though I should have liked him a bit younger. I wasn't sure about the moustache, it was a little too long and looked as if he curled it while he talked. However, the egg without salt, perhaps.

Her clothes were lovely and plentiful, and her dressing-table held a comprehensive selection of the make-up of one of the expensive firms. By the time I'd done her room and opened the door to one or two errand boys I was beginning to feel hungry, and saw with surprise that it was nearly one o'clock. I was amazed at the speed with which time goes when you're working. I thought of the many mornings that I'd spent doing things just to pass the time until lunch, and felt incredibly diligent.

In the afternoon I had to polish the parquet.

I took up all the rugs and moved the furniture back – putting the wax polish on the floor was rather wearing on the knees and stockings, and I began to see that I should have to abandon my principles and wear lisle thread. After that I walked about a mile pushing a broom with a duster tied round it, and it really was most pleasant to see how it polished. I had to keep kneeling down and looking sideways along the floor to see how the sheen was coming up. There was a large area of parquet and it was four o'clock before I'd finished, so I put back the furniture, changed my filthy overalls to a fancy little apron, and made myself a cup of Mrs Baker's black brew.

I was glad to see that Miss Faulkener took the one daily paper that is read in nearly every kitchen all over England. I was able to 'take the weight off me feet' for quite ten minutes, while engrossed in the amusement both intentional and unconscious that it provides, before my mistress arrived demanding tea. I was glad when she revealed some China tea in a tin, because I didn't think the rank black weeds that I had been drinking would suit my constitution for long.

She lit the fire in the drawing-room and I had to persuade her that it was the peculiar direction of the wind and not my inexpert laying that made it belch forth smoke instead of crackling flames. It started to go out altogether, though I knelt in front of it for some time, despairingly holding up a sheet of newspaper with no effect. However, while she was in her bedroom I took the opportunity of getting some methylated spirits from the kitchen and pouring it liberally over the coals. Bravely I threw on a match, and by the time she came back it was crackling away beautifully. She regarded the blue flames a bit suspiciously but said nothing, so I went back to the kitchen to start cooking the dinner. I wasn't going to have a repetition of the Cattermole episode, so I started in good time and tried to figure things out into some sort of order. It was quite a simple dinner, anyway, and she had told me not to put the *soufflé* in till 'Major Nixon' (yes, that sounded like the moustached one) arrived. They would drink their sherry while it was cooking. I appreciated the fact that she realized that a *soufflé* must be waited for and not kept waiting. Miss Faulkener put on a long pale green dinner dress and seemed to be excited. She walked about from room to room, putting on fresh dabs of scent, patting her hair, and puffing up the cushions on the sofa.

As the place was small, the kitchen was not hidden away from the goings-on in the rest of the flat, and I got quite infected with her excitement and felt a thrill myself when the front bell rang.

I took off my cooking apron, and had a look in the glass before flinging open the front door in my best parlour-maid manner.

Yes, it was Moustaches all right, and not bad at that, though his scrutiny of me as I took his hat and coat was a little too intimate. I didn't quite know how to behave. It is rather difficult to be dignified when clad in a short skirt and frilly collar and apron, so I rather hustled him into the drawing-room. His back view was marred by the glimmerings of a bald patch. My *soufflé* was much more fascinating anyway, so I hurried back to the kitchen, and my prayers went with it into the oven. Then I laid the table, lit four green candles, and turned out the lights. The air was pregnant with romance.

Much to my surprise the *soufflé* rose like a bird. When it was nearly cooked I went along to the drawing-room and hung about outside for a bit, saying, 'Dinner is served! Dinner is ready!' to myself to see which sounded best. I finally decided that 'Dinner is served!' can only be done justice to by butlers and the sort of parlour-maids who are called by their surnames.

I said my piece in the intimate manner demanded by the *tête-à-tête* occasion, wrapped a napkin round my *soufflé,* and it was still standing up when I thrust it proudly under Miss Faulkener's nose. I watched anxiously to see how it looked inside, bravely suffering agonies on the hands, as it hadn't occurred to me to put a plate under the dish. She delved delicately in, and revealed it to be miraculously light. Little did she know that it was luck and not judgement that made it so, and she was thrilled, thinking that she had found a really good cook.

The rest of the dinner seemed to go off all right too, though after a time, with wine flowing pretty freely, they were so delighted with each other that anything would have tasted ambrosial.

They were sitting quite close together at the oval table and there was some funny business going on, because I got a hack on the ankle as I came between them to hand him the savoury. I gave them coffee on the sofa in the other half of the room, and, leaving the moustache fairly bristling with anticipation, returned to the disheartening wreckage of the kitchen.

It didn't occur to me in those days to wash up as I went along, not that I would have had time, as cooking took me quite twice as long as it should. I kept doing things wrong and having to rush to cookery books for help, and everything I wanted at a moment's notice had always disappeared. I had hunted round for ages for a wooden spoon, to find it eventually balanced on top of the clock, where I had put it in a moment of abstraction due to a minor crisis. Two minutes later it had gone again, and this time it didn't turn up till the porter of the flats was emptying the dustbin a week later, and asked me if I meant to throw away a perfectly good spoon.

Every saucepan in the place was dirty; the sink was piled high with them. On the floor lay the plates and dishes that couldn't be squeezed on to the table or dresser, already cluttered up with peelings, pudding basins, and dirty little bits of butter.

I didn't feel like eating anything; tasting and picking at oddments as I went along had made me feel rather sick, so I had some coffee, trod on a plate, and started listlessly on the washing-up. The rush and excitement of cooking the dinner, serving it, and watching the progress of *l'amour* had kept me keyed up and energetic. Now that I was alone with the sordid aftermath I suddenly realized how tired I was and that, in the words of the Cattermole cook, 'Me feet were drawing.'

At eleven o'clock I was still at it and my back and head were aching in unison. The washing-up was finished, but the stove was in a hideous mess, and I had got to that stage when one's tired nerves make one feel almost superstitious about anything left undone. I felt I should be run over on the way home or something if I left it dirty till the morning.

Miss Faulkener came in to get some glasses as I was

plying the Vim tin and was horrified to see me still there. 'Goodness, Monica, I thought you'd gone hours ago. Run off now, anyway; you can leave that till tomorrow.'

'Thank you, madam, but I think I'd rather get it done now.'

'Well, just as you like, of course, but if it was me –'

She wafted back to the drawing-room and I thought: 'If it was you, you'd be thinking of how depressing it will be tomorrow morning to arrive at crack of dawn and find things filthy. People may think that by telling you to leave a thing till the next day it will get done magically, all by itself overnight. But no, that is not so, in fact quite the reverse, in all probability it will become a mess of an even greater magnitude.' Exhaustion was making my brain think pedantically. It formed momentous beautifully rounded phrases that meant nothing, as I slaved away automatically. At last I had finished, and, resolutely turning my back on a large spot of grease on the floor, I was washing my hands preparatory to leaving when the pair of them arrived in the kitchen to speed me on my way. Was it my fancy, or did I detect a distinct impatience to be rid of me and have the flat to themselves?

It was, undoubtedly, just normal solicitude for my welfare that made them fairly hustle me out of the front door. I fell into the lift and out again, and propped myself against a lamp-post till my bus arrived. I arrived home in a sort of coma, and if the family were expecting to be regaled with anecdotes of my first day's work they were disappointed. My mother helped me to undress and brought me hot milk, and as I burrowed into the yielding familiarity of my own dear bed, my last thought was thankfulness that I was a 'Daily' and not a 'Liver in'.

Chapter Three

After a week or two at Miss Faulkener's I was beginning to get a bit more efficient, and, therefore, less tired. I was still pretty exhausted by the end of the evening, and it sent me into such an immediate and deep slumber that I felt quite fresh again by the time the alarm clock lifted its voice. I liked the familiarity of my little kitchen and the cooking gave me enormous pleasure. I wasn't so keen on the housework part – though I liked polishing the parquet. I devoted most of my time to it, and it shone with a rare blue gleam. Unfortunately it didn't take Miss Faulkener's attention off other things. Mrs Baker had been right about the finger along the shelves. Life was a wordless and unacknowledged battle of wits between us, with her keeping a sharp look-out for signs of dirt and neglect, and me trying to disguise my slovenliness by subterfuge.

I became an adept at sweeping dust under the bed, and always used the same few pieces of silver, so that I didn't have to keep polishing the rest. Sometimes, if she was in the room while I was making the bed, she would say:

'How about turning the mattress?' She didn't seem to get suspicious of my always answering: 'I turned it only yesterday madam,' so somehow I don't think the thing was turned all the time I was there. It was much too heavy, anyway.

If she was in the mood she would chat to me very amusingly. My conversation, naturally, was limited, as it had to be discreetly deferential, and I couldn't start talking unless she did, or stay in a room after she had finished what she wanted to say.

A maid makes a good defenceless listener for people who want to talk about themselves and not be answered back.

Any repression this may have caused me to feel was fully made up for by the social whirl of the back door. I was getting to know all the tradesmen so well that I felt as if I had been in the place for years. The milkman, who suspected his wife of carrying on with a travelling salesman, often dropped in for a cup of tea and a bit of advice on how to treat women, but my real pal was the 'Grosher'. He was a pools maniac, and he got me so infected with his enthusiasm that, with his assistance, I took it up.

His was the first finger every morning to give me the nerve storm still produced by that dreadful bell. I would give him the orders first, before I forgot, and then we would get down to the more important business of selection, interrupted here and there by reminiscences of his pools experiences.

'When I won shixteen poundsh by a lucky shot with me four awaysh' was an anecdote I never got tired of hearing, or he of telling. Despite the fact that it was two years ago, and he hadn't won a penny since, we were not disheartened. Thursday mornings, when he helped me to fill in my form, were grim and earnest affairs, involving much heavy breathing and licking of a short stump of pencil.

'Arshenal, Mish? Never touch 'em meshelf. Chelshea neither, for that matter – too variable. Put a cross in 'ere – *sho,* heresh away win – *sho*,' as we put in the last mystic sign. 'That ought to bring us home thish week. Gawd shave us if that new centre forward isn't worth his prysh money.'

Monday morning found us slightly damped but not discouraged, and we would discuss with undaunted optimism the new week's chances. Dear 'Grosher'! I wonder whether he has ever repeated his historic success. I gave up the pools when I went elsewhere, as I couldn't do them without him. Whenever football is mentioned I think of bicycling clips; it keeps his memory green.

Miss Faulkener seemed to have a great many friends, and she often went to lunch and cocktail parties. Her evenings were mostly dedicated to Major Nixon. When he didn't come to dinner at the flat they would go out together – she very gay with orchids and glamorously scented.

I was becoming such a familiar piece of furniture about the place by this time that they didn't always bother to address their remarks in French when I was in the room.

One day, while I was handing them some rather choice grilled kidneys, she said: 'Darling, I think we ought to give a cocktail party.'

'Why, my sweet, we don't want a whole lot of frightful people all over the place.'

'No, but I think we ought. I owe a lot of people, and it would be rather fun. Monica could make us some attractive things to eat, couldn't you, Monica?'

'Certainly, madam.'

'Let's fix a date.'

'Must we, darling? I tell you I don't like the idea of people barging around our dear little flat – I like to have you to myself here.'

He laid a tender hand on her arm.

'*Pas devant la bonne, chérie.*'

I didn't always slide tactfully out of the room when they said that. I wasn't going to let on that I knew French, because they sometimes said entertaining things which they thought I didn't understand.

The party date was fixed and I was given piles of half-penny stamped envelopes to post on my way home. It was going to be rather a crush, if everyone accepted, even with most of the furniture turned out of the double room.

Looking through the names, I discovered to my horror that she had invited a couple I knew. Even if I warned them beforehand, they were a most indiscreet pair and would be sure to embarrass me horribly.

I had to search through the letters on her desk every day when she wasn't looking to see if they had accepted. I was greatly relieved when I discovered a letter saying that they were away and would be unable to come. I just got the letter back in time to be dusting busily as she came into the room. Pool discussions were postponed while I ordered a large supply of drink and various cocktail accessories from the 'grosher'.

I spent nearly all the day of the party making cheese straws, sausage rolls, sandwiches, and other oddments, and thought it a good excuse not to do any more housework than the bare essentials. Moustaches arrived at tea-time, and the pair of them came into the kitchen to make the cocktails. We were all very merry, and they had their tea sitting on the kitchen table, feeling as if they were doing a bit of slumming. I regaled them with imaginary anecdotes of other employers, and they did a lot of tasting the cocktails; by the time they had finished they were so mellow that they gave me one.

They went off, giggling like a couple of schoolchildren. I think they thought I would get drunk on it.

She went to get dressed, and I spread out the food and drink in tasteful array, while Major Nixon was out getting cigarettes. I didn't much care for the idea of being alone in a room with him. I had a new apron for the occasion and a coy ribbon in the hair. The guests would probably be too taken up with the impression they were going to create to notice me when I opened the door, but still, one has one's pride.

The hostess, suitably enough, wore what is known as a 'Hostess Gown'. A lovely clinging dress of cherry red which made her look almost frighteningly sophisticated. The host wore a red carnation and his most debonair manner. The porter of the flats was 'obliging' in a smart white coat. He was to hand the drinks, and I had to open the door, take coats and hats, offer the ladies the bedroom, and announce the names. This was quite a business as, after the first trickle of people, everybody seemed to arrive at once, and I went back and forth like a shuttle between the front door and the drawing-room. Some of the guests had the most extraordinary sounding names, or else I didn't hear properly – people do mumble so, and you can't very well ask them to repeat themselves more than once. I had a shot at them all, but some of them sounded even more extraordinary when announced by me in loud but refined accents.

The party seemed to be going very well. Major Nixon helped the porter with handing the drinks and I must say the pair of them were very efficient. Everyone got all they wanted and more, and the noise rose to great height. Miss Faulkener did her stuff well, too, willowing from one person to another, introducing people, and having a word here and there with everyone. 'My dear, how *lovely* to see you again. How *are* you? And John too?'

'I *adore* your hat, Alice – Paris? It looks like it – Basil, you simply *must* meet a most attractive girl I've asked specially for you.' And so on, after the same manner of all cocktail parties. Once I looked in from the hall, and she was talking to someone rather abstractedly, and shooting irritable glances to where the moustache was being at its most fascinating in conversation with a glamorous red-head. When people started to go I got a bit muddled up with the coats and tried to palm off hats on them that were much too small, but they didn't seem to mind, so it didn't really matter. One woman was a bit annoyed because I had put her gloves in the wrong coat pocket, and someone else had gone off with them, but luckily her husband got tired of waiting while she made a fuss and hustled her off.

At last even the hangers-on had been almost pushed out by the hostess, who was looking forward to the *tête-à-tête* celebration at a restaurant that she and Major Nixon had planned. He was rather loath to let the red-head go, but Miss Faulkener manoeuvred her safely away. When everybody had gone she vented a slight irritation on him by cursing him for keeping her waiting when she was ready to go, thanked the porter and me, and swept out with the moustache escorting her sulkily, several yards in the rear.

The porter had a quick swig of some cocktail that was left and descended to his *True Story Magazine* on the chair by the main door. I rushed to the telephone as I had arranged with a friend of mine that I would ring her up as soon as everyone had gone and she would come and help me clear up the mess. She was waiting at a house quite near by, and didn't take long to come round. Our hearts quailed before the amount of debris, so we decided to fortify ourselves first. Isobel went round the room collecting all the drink left in shakers and glasses while I made a choice selection of food, and we had a very good party all to ourselves in the kitchen. After a bit we felt in much too good form to apply ourselves to washing up, but it had to be done, so we turned on the wireless and accompanied our labours with song. We didn't break much, but it's a curious fact that good glass cracks at a touch, while cheap stuff can be hurled about with perfect safety. We were only about half finished, and luckily were singing a *pianissimo* phrase when I heard a key in the lock. There was no time to turn off the wireless, but I was just able to push Isobel out on to the back staircase before Miss Faulkener walked in with a face like thunder. 'Not done yet?' she said as I appeared from the kitchen wearing an expression of innocent inquiry.

'I'm getting on, thank you, madam.'

'Well, be as quick as you can, and turn off the wireless – I've got a splitting head.' She banged into her bedroom before I could apologize about the wireless, so I switched it off and quietly let Isobel in again. She appeared still clutching a dishcloth and a plate, and we finished the work sketchily and could only speculate in whispers as to what they had quarrelled about.

Moustaches would get hell for it tomorrow anyway, for she was a woman who could be quite charming when she chose, but perfectly intolerable when roused.

Luckily for him, he did the right thing by sending a huge box of roses in the morning and arriving at half past six in a white tie with orchids and theatre tickets and a table booked at the Savoy.

She had been to bed early the night before, so her liver was in good order, and she evidently forgave him, for she went and dressed, and they went off together most amicably.

After this the days rolled on uneventfully for some time, marked only by such high spots as pay-day, and discovering how to make Welsh Rarebit. There were a few contretemps, of course, such as the day when I decided to clean the stove and took it all to bits and couldn't put it together again. We had to have the gas man in before Miss Faulkener could have so much as a cup of tea. He also solved the mystery for me of why the ice in the refrigerator was always melting. He roared with uncouth laughter when he realized that I didn't know that one had to keep the door shut.

Apart from such slight matters as these kitchen life went smoothly, and so did life 'above stairs', but it was not to last.

One evening Major Nixon arrived to fetch Miss Faulkener, distinctly the worse for alcohol. She was in her bedroom so she didn't hear him greet me with 'Hullo, Sweetheart!' when I let him in. I ignored it and stalked away to go on with what I was doing. He came into the kitchen while I was mixing some dough at the table with my back to the door. A beery breath whistled over my shoulder as he implanted the merest suspicion of a kiss on the back of my neck. I thought it would be more dignified to pretend I hadn't noticed, so I went on mixing.

'Have we got any gin?' he asked, going over to the cupboard. I indicated the bottle, and when he turned round with it in his hand I saw that he was wearing the repulsive leer that some men keep for women of a lower order.

'I didn't really come here for gin, my dear,' he said, advancing on me, and before I had time to take my hands out of the dough he clutched me to him in a very unrefined embrace.

A voice of icy calm spoke from the doorway: 'I am ready to go, John, whenever you are.'

It was true to the best novelette standards. He released me hurriedly and trailed out after Miss Faulkener. Not a word was spoken, and I heard the front door bang as I went on with my mixing.

I was scared stiff of meeting my mistress the next morning. She was awake and sitting up in bed when I took in her breakfast.

She was courtesy itself as she explained to me that she was suddenly obliged to go away and would therefore no longer require my services.

'I shall be going at once, so I will give you a week's wages in lieu of notice and you can go today.'

'Yes, madam, thank you,' I whispered. I felt terribly crushed and guilty. I hadn't expected quite such drastic retribution for something that was really not my fault. She went out early (to look for another maid I suppose), and, though I could see she was livid inside, she was well bred to the last, and we parted with a chilly but civilized handshake.

It took me the best part of the day to clear up the flat, and leave things tidy, which I felt was the least I could do. I arrived home in the middle of a dinner party and had a great success with the story of my disgrace, which I exaggerated a bit so as not to make it too ignominious.

Expulsion of any sort always seems to tickle the sense of humour. It had been just the same when I was thrown out of the Dramatic School, and before that when my school authorities told me that I could not attend any more if I persisted in my refusal to wear the school hat. Staying in bed the next morning was lovely, but, much to my surprise, I began to feel restive about lunch-time and itching for a bit of work. I had not yet had my fill of manual labour, so I trailed off again to the agency in my special job-hunting hat.

I gave the agency a fundamentally true but prejudiced story of my dismissal, vindicating my honour completely, and the woman took it well. She thought it a pity that I had not got a reference, but was sure that she could fix me up again at once. It seemed that one need never be unemployed, as the demand for cook-generals greatly exceeded the supply. She gave me three numbers to ring up, and I went out very excited at the thought of starting on a new and possibly exciting phase of my career. One of the numbers was that of the London editor of an American paper. I dialled that first as I thought it might be fun to see a bit of life among the journalists.

'*American Post* speaking – Mr Feldbaum's secretary,' said a brisk voice, American in its efficiency but Tooting in its accent.

'I wish to inquire about the post as cook-general in Mr Feldbaum's flat.'

'What experience and qualifications have you, please?'

Drawing largely on my imagination, I gave her the

works, and she told me that I could go round to the office and see Mr Feldbaum at once.

I had got myself a shillingsworth of pennies, so I thought I might as well ring up the other numbers while I was in the box. The next shot was a Miss Jones-Haweson of West Kensington.

I said: 'With reference to the post of cook-general –' She said: 'Thank you, I am already suited.'

I said, ' Oh,' and we rang off.

Short and to the point, but a waste of twopence. The third name that the agency had given me was Martin Parrish, Esq., of a Campden Hill address. The name seemed vaguely familiar, but I couldn't think in what connexion. A petulant voice answered the telephone, but he sounded quite hopeful, so I arranged to go and see him after I had been up to the city to see Mr Feldbaum.

The London headquarters of the *American Post* seethed with activity, but they were not imposing. One enormous room, with as many desks as possible crammed in jigsaw fashion, comprised the whole outfit.

The editor's office was a minute square in one corner, divided from the commotion by two thin pieces of match-boarding which didn't even reach to the ceiling. It was possibly due to the fact that one had to shout to be heard above the rattling typewriters that Mr Feldbaum's conversation was monosyllabic. He was completely bald. He looked very surprised when I was shown in, and raised the place where his eyebrows should have been. I sat down on the edge of a hard, narrow chair, and we gazed at one another in silence for a bit.

'Mm,' he said at last, 'very young.'

'Oh, but this isn't my first place, sir. Were you wanting someone a little older?'

'Mm – much older woman – I'm a bachelor. People will talk.'

It was my turn to look surprised. I thought I looked drab enough 'in me Blacks' to stop any gossip. I didn't know what to say, so I just sat while he pondered over me, and the typewriters filled the silence between us with their clicking. Eventually he said:

'What can you do?' So I embarked on my usual recital of self-praise, but it didn't seem to make much impression. He had already made up his mind. 'So sorry,' he said. 'Pity.' Though not eloquent, he was very polite and I was sorry too. However, I had another string to my bow, so took myself off quite jauntily. I had a little difficulty in finding Martin Parrish's house. It was in one of those ex-slum streets that have been converted into dear little bijou residences with window-boxes and red front doors. I roamed round the neighbourhood of Notting Hill Gate for quite a time, and when at last I found it, I was quite thankful to sit down on the chair that Martin Parrish offered me. Though I didn't much care for the looks of him – he was short and pink-faced with soft yellow hair and a little snapdragon mouth – he seemed quite pleased to see me. In my innocence, I thought this was a good sign, so when he offered me thirty shillings a week I jumped at it. Heaving his plump body out of an armchair, he showed me over the house. I began to think I quite liked him. He was affably polite, and very anxious that I should like everything, and at first sight it seemed a pleasant enough job. The house was tiny, with the drawing-room and bathroom on the top floor, dining-room and bedroom below, and kitchen in the basement at the bottom of a steep narrow flight of stairs. I had no time for more than a cursory glance over things, as Mr Parrish suddenly caught sight of a clock and gave a yelp.

'Good heavens – I'd no idea it was so late. I'm supposed to be miles away from here in ten minutes' time. I must fly.' He explained about his breakfast, and one or two minor whims, and the whole thing seemed fairly simple. I was glad that the misgivings of Mr Feldbaum didn't seem to have crossed his mind. The only snag to an otherwise pleasant prospect was that although he didn't want his breakfast early, he wanted me to get there at eight o'clock in the morning.

'Mimi wakes at eight, and likes to be let out, poor darling. You haven't met Mimi, have you? I do so hope you're fond of Pekes.'

'Yes, sir, I adore them,' I said, crossing my thumbs to eradicate the lie.

'Well, then, that's settled. Now I must rush; and you'll be sure to come in good time tomorrow – splendid.' We parted, and I went home and early to bed, setting my alarm clock at an even more ungodly hour than before.

I was dying to find out in what connexion I had heard the name of Martin Parrish, so the first thing I did when I arrived next morning was to rummage among the papers in the streamlined desk which stood in one corner of the drawing-room. It didn't take long to discover that he was a dress designer and writer of fashion articles for various magazines. Of course! Now I recalled how I had heard of him: 'Martin Parrish designs a glamorously Edwardian ball dress for our readers.' '"Stripes and ultra-smart and entrancingly gay," says Martin Parrish.' 'Martin Parrish shows you how to add sophistication to the "little black dress".' I was startled out of my investigations by a bell even shriller than the one at Miss Faulkener's, and rushing to look at the indicator in the kitchen, found a little red arrow agitating madly in the space marked 'bedroom'.

The first thing that struck me (literally) as I entered my master's room was the atmosphere. It practically knocked me down, but I recovered, reeling, and saw that he had gone to sleep with the window shut and the electric fire on. He was sitting up in bed, unappetizingly tousled.

'Mimi's been asking to go out for hours – she woke me up,' he grumbled. 'You're pretty late. Still – as it's your first morning –' There was a heaving under the bedclothes, and a dirty brown ball of fur scrambled up and took off from Martin's chest to land on mine with yelps of joy or hatred.

'There! She likes you, that's splendid. Take the darling down and let her out.' He thumped down under the bedclothes and pulled the sheets over his head, and I slung the darling into the street, praying that she might never return, and went back to the kitchen. Now that I had time for a proper inspection, I began to see that, although the rest of the house had been done up in a modern fashion, the kitchen had been rather skimped – the stove was evidently an old one from another house and was encrusted with the grease and spillings of years. The dresser was only half made; there were no doors to the cupboards underneath it; there was no plate-rack, and no grooves in the draining board.

My eye observed these things with misgiving, for by such little details is kitchen life governed. I opened a few drawers and saw that there was also a distinct shortage of utensils. I wondered if my predecessor had cooked, like the Maltese, entirely with the aid of her hands. However, the walls and woodwork were freshly painted and the red tiled floor was nice. I decided that if the dress designer would let me have, perhaps, a bit of stuff left over from Lady Whatsit's trousseau for curtains, this room, the hub and focus of my existence, might not be so bad.

Better still, if I could get rid of the various broken jugs, vases, cardboard boxes, and other junk which were piled on the mantelpiece and the top of the cupboard and dresser. Mr Parrish had evidently mistaken the kitchen for a lumber room.

He didn't want his breakfast till about ten o'clock, so I had plenty of time to lay the drawing-room fire and do a little dusting. The carpet was a new one, and when in a fit of enthusiasm I started to brush it the pile came off in great furry lumps and made more mess than before. If that was what was going to happen when I expended a little extra zeal, I wasn't going to waste my energy, so I left it to its fate and went downstairs to start burning toast and over-boiling eggs for Martin's breakfast.

When I took it up he had gone to sleep again, so I took the opportunity to open the window surreptitiously, glancing at the bed to see whether the blessed little breath of air would upset him. All I could see was a few matted hairs sticking out of the top of the round hump under the bed-clothes. There was no sign of life, so I was just going quietly out when the telephone rang. I went back to the bed and answered it. He woke and heaved himself up to mumble into it in a doped sort of way when I handed it to him, then an unfamiliar presence smote his consciousness.

'For God's sake, shut that damned window,' he moaned to me. 'No, not you, Norman,' into the telephone, 'I'm in the most frightful draught, that's all.' I gave a bitter laugh inside myself and swept from the room.

Shortly afterwards I had to brave the gas-chamber again, to ask whether there was any food to be ordered.

He was still in bed, and I took up my stand by the window while he consulted a messy note-book, so loose-leaved that pages kept fluttering out and had to be retrieved from under the bed.

'My secretary will be here to lunch, so we shall be two; three tonight, as a lady and gentleman are coming.' He lay back against the pillows and deliberated, and I felt it might be a good thing to make an impression by rattling off suggestions in a proficient way. This was a mistake as it gave him *illusions de grandeur*, and he chose an elaborate dinner that was going to be quite a strain to cope with.

I was glad to hear that the tradesmen called, though I thought it wouldn't have done his figure any harm to trot round the shops.

'Order what you need. There may be one or two things you like to have in stock. We've only just moved in, so I'm afraid the kitchen isn't quite fully equipped.'

I took advantage of this understatement to clarify the need for a few essentials such as sieves, spoons, saucepans, etc.

'Well, you'd better get those yourself. I'll give you some money and you can pop round to Woolworth's some time – you can get out every afternoon between lunch and tea; by the way, I think people ought to get all the fresh air they can.' I refrained from saying: 'Then why sleep with your window shut?' and left the room, as I could hear faint cries of 'Milko!' from the street. The milkman wasn't nearly as nice as the one with the unfaithful wife. I went out to give his pony some sugar and discovered that they were both bad tempered. One cursed me for not putting out the empties and the other bit me.

There was no sign of Martin getting up, so I couldn't contemplate doing his room yet. Anyhow, I could hear the faint strains of the bell from below, and I ran downstairs to find the arrow bouncing at 'Back door'. I began to see why people have to move into flats because they can't get maids for their houses. However, running up and down stairs may be death to the arches of the feet, but it is very good for the figure.

The greengrocer was a perfect Adonis, but not talkative. I gave him a string of orders and an allusion to the weather, and his sole contribution to the conversation was 'Ah'.

'Beautiful but dumb,' I thought as he sped off on his bicycle like a Greek charioteer. 'Still, you can't have everything.' Looking through the store cupboard, I found it contained practically nothing but salt and pepper and a few old tins of cocoa, permanently sealed with rust and age. I had been told to order what I needed, so I made out a long list for the grocer, and was in the middle of dictating it to him when the bell rang from upstairs. I thrust the list into his trembling hands – he was an ancient grocer of the high collar era – and panted up to the top floor.

Mr Parrish was out of bed and wrapped in another of the flowery garments that he favoured – a sort of kimono this time.

'Please light the drawing-room fire so that the room can warm up before I go down,' he said. After I had done that I heard sounds of him going to his bath, so I thought I might as well make his bed. The pillow was smeary with grease and the sheets were covered with Mimi's dirty hairs. The bell rang while I was fighting down the nausea that this aroused in me, and after having toiled all the way down to the basement, only to find that it was the front bell this time, I opened the door on a very nice young man indeed.

'Whom did you wish to see?' I said.

'I am Mr Parrish's secretary,' he said with a shy smile, tapping the brief case under his arm. He went into the drawing-room to wait for his employer. Something about his gentle boyishness appealed to my maternal affection, so I poked up the fire for him and said there was a nip in the air, before returning to my bed-making. I thought Mr Parrish was still in the bath, so I walked into the bedroom without knocking and surprised the gentleman in long woollen pants.

'Monica,' he said, in a controlled but cutting voice, 'it is not considered manners to enter a bedroom without knocking. Please remember this.'

I didn't think it was worth while explaining, so I retired with dignity. When eventually he was out of his room it was time to start the lunch, so I left the bed, meaning to do it in the intervals of cooking, but, somehow, what with one thing and another there were no intervals. Bells rang, sauces boiled over, the spinach took hours to wash and prepare, and as there were so few saucepans I had to keep washing them.

The first opportunity I had to get upstairs was when I had handed round the first course and shut the door on the sounds of eating. I raced up, and just had time to do the bed before the dining-room bell sent me flying down again. Mr Parrish wanted a second helping it seemed. This was surprising in view of the fact that he had done nothing in the short time since eating a hearty breakfast, except lie in bed or recline on a sofa dictating a few letters.

I just had time while they were on the next course to go back again and flick around with a duster, removing cigarette ash and talcum powder, to make the rooms at least look as if I'd done them. I had made the mistake of doing the bathroom before Martin Parrish was up, and he had turned the place into a dripping shambles, so my good work had gone for naught. A shambles it remained, for 'they' were screaming for coffee and my stomach was screaming for food.

It was half past two before I eventually relaxed over the dried-up remains of the lunch that had been keeping warm in the oven.

I had only shovelled down one or two mouthfuls in the unladylike manner that one employs when tired, hungry, and alone, when the red arrow started to do the rumba under 'Drawing-room'. I went upstairs chewing, and discovered that they wanted more coffee, and I wondered when they were going to get down to a little serious designing – they certainly did not look like it at the moment.

When I had finished my lunch I lit a cigarette, and putting my feet upon the table as there was only one chair, I 'took time off', resolutely shutting my mind to dishes that wanted washing. Let bells ring themselves hoarse all round me, I was on strike for five minutes.

Chapter Four

Now that I had time to reflect at leisure on my new situation I came to a great many conclusions. The chief one was that now that Mr Parrish had got a maid safely installed he was a changed man. He was still quite friendly, but that affable solicitude for my happiness had rather worn off. I realized that there was more than enough work for one person to do in this house, and that I would have to bring all my labour-saving ingenuity into play to cope with it. He had said that I could go out every afternoon if I liked, so after I had washed up the lunch things I thought I might make a little trek to Woolworth's to buy what I needed. I was just climbing out of my uniform when the drawing-room bell rang and I had to climb back into it and run upstairs. The secretary was typing in a dilettante way, while the designer sat on the sofa with a large board on his knee – presumably designing.

Holding up the top of my apron with one hand, as I hadn't had time to find a pin, I inquired what they wanted. The creative genius was suspended for a moment while he said: 'A lady is coming to tea at half past four. Could you make us some scones and little cakes, or something?'

'With pleasure, sir.'

'Thank you so much.' He threw me a fascinating smile, as if he knew that I would not now have time to go out and was trying to placate me. When he was once more safely immersed in his drawing I responded with an ironical leer and returned below.

Making cakes is not my strong point, especially with very few materials at hand and no cake-tins. However, I managed to throw together some fairly passable rock cakes and short-bread, and made a few surprisingly successful scones with a tin of Ideal milk. I thought I might as well make enough to keep them quiet for a few days so that I could be sure of getting out one afternoon in the near future. It was getting quite dark by half past four, always a cosy time of day, and the kitchen, which was beautifully warm and smelt pleasantly of baking, would have been quite snug if I had had some curtains to draw.

Feeling quite happy, I went upstairs to answer the front door bell, and admitted a competent-looking girl, fashionably dressed, though a trifle spotty about the face, carrying a large brown paper parcel. When I took in the tea the drawing-room was draped in lengths of material of all colours, and the three of them were flinging themselves among it, holding up a piece here and there and exclaiming ecstatically. I put the tea-tray down on a vacant stool and was just going out when Martin Parrish rushed at me with a bit of gold *lamé*, and, commanding me to stand still, draped it swiftly and skilfully round my form. He stepped back with clasped hands, surveying with his head on one side, and I stood there feeling like one of those improbable-looking effigies in shop windows.

'Look!' he cried, calling upon the other two to admire. 'Quite perfect for that blonde type – the whole effect in gold could be *too* marvellous. Take a note, Kenneth; what's the number of the stuff? Oh, yes. Here – avoid any contrasts with BX 17 – accessories, etc., unbroken line important to carry on colour effect. Oh, wait – how about this?' Very excited, he wound something dark red round my middle, only to tear it off again impatiently – pushing me about dispassionately as if I really were canvas and sawdust.

'Ah, delicious!' they all cried when the desired effect had been obtained. I wanted to go and put the joint in the oven and started to edge towards the door when the *lamé* was unpinned.

'No, don't go away, I haven't finished,' said my employer irritably as he advanced on me with a length of black taffeta which he bunched round me, crying: 'The classic contrast! You can't get away from it!' I began to think I might soon ask for a rise. He was quite carried away by his art and had evidently forgotten that I was only the cook and had better things to do than stand around all day being draped. I wished I had a union which would forbid me to act as a model during working hours. Eventually he became absorbed in a discussion with Kenneth, the secretary; and, having also discovered the cakes, they were quite happy waving them about in the air and talking with their mouths full. I seized the opportunity, while I was temporarily forgotten, to escape to the kitchen and start preparing the dinner.

I took a great deal of trouble over it as I wanted to make an impression on my first day. I got along quite well, in spite of being interrupted by summonses from above – the first time to clear the tea. I saw my employer looking at me meditatively while he fingered a piece of blue chiffon, so I fairly skipped out of the room with the tray before he could pounce. The next time it was to help the spotty girl fold up the stuff, and yet again when she and Kenneth had gone, to make up the fire and bring sherry.

The guests were a little late, luckily, otherwise the dinner would not have been ready. They were Americans, she rather loud-voiced and voluble and he a little quiet man with a sad smile, and a glance for me round the corner of his pince-nez. I tried out 'Dinner is served' on them in a vain attempt to better myself, but the effect was rather spoiled by the door-knob coming off in my hand as I said it. Evidently the kitchen wasn't the only room in the house that was lacking in efficient construction, and Mr Parrish said 'tch, tch,' and glared at me as if it was my fault. I replaced the handle apologetically and took the tattered remnants of my dignity downstairs. They followed close on my heels, and I handed round the soup, justly proud of its creamy smoothness. 'He' had asked for *potage bonne femme*, so I had made it in its most superior form, sparing neither cream nor eggs. The American woman was smoking so I placed an ash-tray beside her, but to my horror she did not put out her cigarette but held it in her left hand, taking puffs in between almost every mouthful of soup. I was terribly upset and moved the ash-tray a little nearer as I passed, but she was talking and didn't notice.

The next course was *oeufs mornay*. One of the eggs was rather overcooked and shrivelled, so I put it at the end, and handed her the dish so that she would be pretty sure to take that one. She did so, waving a freshly-lighted cigarette over the other eggs and ate it abstractedly, so that I was tempted to give her boot polish instead of anchovy for the savoury, to see if she would notice. Having learnt my lesson at Miss Faulkener's, I washed up as much as I could as I went along, but it was an unequal struggle. Some of the things had to be cooked while they were eating the course before, and the end of dinner found me exhausted and surrounded by almost every plate we had in stock, all dirty. I took up the coffee and tried to send a telepathic hate wave to the American woman, which can't have reached her, for her hand never faltered as she lit a fresh cigarette from the stub of her last. I ploughed through the washing-up, fury lending speed if not deftness to my hands, and stacked the dishes in the doorless cupboards where they would rapidly collect the dust again. Then I slung a few odd bits of broken china into the huge inverted electric light bowl which did duty as a rubbish bin, and left the premises by my private route – the area steps – not forgetting to put out the milk bottles.

The next morning Mr Parrish's first words to me were:

'You must not rush off like that without letting me know; we might want something before you go. Last night I had some letters I wanted you to post.'

The morning followed much the same course as the day before, except that about eleven o'clock I answered the front door to a small brisk man with a neat moustache who wanted to sell me a vacuum cleaner. I thought this was a very good idea; it would save me a lot of work and give me endless amusement. He gave me a card which said: 'E. L. Robbins, representative "Sucka" vacuum cleaners,' so I left him in the hall and went upstairs to give my employer a short résumé of his sales talk. It went down quite well, and I managed half to convince him that no house could possibly be kept properly without a vacuum cleaner and that it saved expense in the long run.

'I'm wasted as a servant – a commercial traveller's what I ought to have been,' I thought as I went downstairs to tell the man that Mr Parrish would see him in the drawing-room. He had gone in there already, which I thought was rather presumptuous, and I gave a hasty glance round to see whether he'd pinched any cigarette-boxes or anything. Not that I really cared whether the dress designer was robbed of his trinkets, but they might suspect me.

He was quite a long time coming, and as I couldn't see anything missing I unbent towards E. L. Robbins and we had quite a cosy little chat.

He told me all about the vagaries of door-to-door life. 'Ever so nice, some are,' he said, fingering his Old (high) School tie. 'Talk away for hours, as pleasant as you please – even give you a cup of tea.' If this was a hint I ignored it. 'Then at the end they break it to you that a vacuum cleaner is the last thing in the world they'd think of buying, and there you are. A morning wasted, and what to show for it? Nothing. No, reely I'd rather they'd slam the door in your face at once like some do – ever so rude. Time is money *I* say.'

'Well, I hope you'll be able to persuade him to buy one of your thingammies here,' I said. 'It'll be a great help to me – there's so much to do, and he expects me to be a human dynamo.'

'No, reely? What a crying shame.'

'Yes, honestly – do you know –'

Here we launched off, with one eye on the door, into a wonderful gossip, he registering suitable horror and sympathy as I unfolded an exaggerated account of my hardships.

'Put upon you are, my dear – that's what I say.' At this point I suddenly recollected that perhaps there is such a thing as loyalty to one's employer, and I didn't much care for the 'my dear' or the too sympathetic gleam in his bulging eye. Anyway, I could hear the flop-flop of bedroom slippers descending the stairs, so I took myself off as Martin Parrish entered in a black dressing-gown with a gold dragon on the back. I left them to it, and the result was that Mr Parrish consented to see a demonstration. I was summoned from the kitchen to attend, and Kenneth arrived while the parts were being fitted together, so Mr Robbins had quite an audience as he trotted briskly about with his machine, sucking up quantities of dust from the most astonishing places.

It was a great success. He fairly brought down the house by blowing a current of air under the carpet to 'freshen away the damp', which made it bulge and billow like a gentle sea. Mr Parrish and Kenneth conferred together while the machine was being dismantled, and the upshot of it was that they decided to buy a small one on the hire-purchase system, which, expounded by E. L. Robbins, sounded almost too reasonable. When he had gone I went down to answer the back door to my dream greengrocer, who was much chattier this morning and actually delivered himself of the information that lettuces were fourpence each.

I felt in quite good spirits today. My employer had been roused out of his morning torpor by the vacuum cleaner, so I was actually able to do the bedroom and bathroom after lunch. I didn't waste much time on them; I thought the dirt could wait till tomorrow, when it could be sucked neatly away. They were going to have cold meat and salad for lunch, and were going out to dinner, so I got down to a bit of cleaning in the kitchen. The floor was filthy, so I went on my hands and knees and scrubbed it. I started by the door, so as to be able to get fresh water from the sink without treading on the clean part, but this turned out to be not such a good plan. The back door bell kept ringing and I had to raise myself creaking and groaning and paddle over a morass to answer it. I was distinctly short with the tradesmen – they seemed to be doing it on purpose, and the milkman gave me back as good as he got.

'Keep yer bleedin' 'air on, if you call it 'air,' was his brilliant parting shot.

'The only way I can tell you and your horse apart is the

horse is better looking,' I shouted after him up the area steps. Not scintillating, but good enough by dairy standards. So, quite satisfied, I waded back to where I had left off scrubbing. When I had finished my arms were streaked with grey to above the elbows, and as I had taken the precaution of removing my stockings, my legs were in the same state. I thought I had better wash before handing round the lunch, so I shut myself in the bathroom and scrubbed with the best scented soap. I didn't hear Martin trying the door as the tap was running, and when I came out he was hovering about irritably and intimated to me that the kitchen sink was the proper place in which to clean my vile body. I swelled with class consciousness, but said nothing and retired below, leaving a trail of 'Ashes of Roses' in my wake.

After lunch I got myself dirty all over again cleaning the stove, so as a protest I didn't bother to wash before taking up the tea. Mr Parrish stared very hard at a large smudge on my cheek and the black borders of my fingernails, but decided not to waste his breath on me. I was able to go soon after that as he was going out. I laid the breakfast tray all ready so as to save time in the morning. I was pleased with the results of my field day in the kitchen. It was looking very trim, and I discovered a gloomy insect-ridden hole under the stairs where I stacked all the old vases and rubbish. Needless to say, I had no sooner done this than Mr Parrish came clattering down the stairs looking for 'that iridescent glass bowl that I put on top of the dresser'.

He exclaimed at the unaccustomed tidiness and was pleased, I think, but he said: 'Oh, dear, what have you done with all that stuff I put in here to be out of the way? Not thrown it away, I hope?'

'Oh, no, sir, I put it in a cupboard. It did catch the dust so. I'll soon get it for you.'

I unearthed it while he fiddled around on a tour of inspection in the kitchen.

'Didn't you know that you mustn't keep marmalade in an open bowl? It ought to be kept in the pot and just turned into the bowl when it's wanted. Oh! and you oughtn't to squeeze the orange juice overnight, even if you do put it in the frig. It loses its vitamins, you see. What became of that tin of milk that was in the cupboard?'

'I used it to make scones, sir.'

'Oh, dear, I was keeping it for Mimi. She does so love it. *Ought* you to have used it for scones? Were they all right? I always think it gives things a tinny flavour when cooked.'

All this was said in quite a tolerant if patronizing way. He really meant to educate me quite kindly, and he may have known more about things than I did – certainly no one could have known less, but I began to understand how our old cook at home felt when she guarded 'her' kitchen in that proprietary way. Anyway, a man shouldn't interfere with domestic details.

'In fact, a cook's what you're turning into, mentally and physically,' I thought as I pulled my gloves over my work-soiled hands and flapped off to Woolworth's on my dropped arches.

I arrived the next morning with my arms full of brown paper bags containing all I needed to make kitchen life happy. I had only spent about six shillings, but it had cleared me out, as it was a long time since pay-day, so when I went up for my master to order the food, I mentioned quite casually in the course of conversation what I had spent.

'You rather let yourself go, didn't you?'

'Well, sir, they were really all things I had to have.' I enumerated them, and though he tut-tutted a bit he couldn't dispute it.

'I don't seem to have any change. Well, never mind. I'll give it you another time. Now about lunch. I shall be alone as my secretary doesn't come today. I shall be out for tea. I have a gentleman coming to dinner. I thought perhaps we might have a chicken, some soup to start with, and perhaps a sweet omelette, plenty of jam. I like that. Oh, heavens! Don't tell me that's Mimi!'

A terrible yelping was corning from outside accompanied by shrill barks. Mr Parrish shot out of bed, and we both rushed to the window. Mr Parrish nearly fainted with horror. Mimi was standing on the top step, snarling and yapping, and looking even more objectionable than usual, while in the street a small terrier was jumping up and down, barking with frenzied rage at the Peke.

'Oh, run down at once and get poor Mimi!' wailed Martin, so down I had to go and pick up the crazy thing, at great peril to my own skin, and take it indoors, holding it tightly round the middle.

'All right, all right, I sympathize with you,' I said to the terrier who was jumping up my legs, and shutting the front door in his enraged face. I took Mimi upstairs to her anguished father. The climax was reached when we discovered a drop of blood on her chest, and even when, after an exhaustive search, we discovered it must have been the other dog's blood, he was still not appeased.

'I'd no idea you just put her out in the street and left her all on her own. You ought to stay and watch her till she's had her little run and then bring her in. You never know *what* may happen in London.'

'No, really,' I thought, 'this is too much – a model, perhaps, but *not* a Peke's nursemaid.'

Aloud I said: 'I'm very sorry, sir, but I'm afraid I really wouldn't have time in the mornings to stop after that.'

'Well then you must *make* time.' This remark was so ridiculous that I couldn't even bother to answer it, so I put Mimi down on the bed and left the room in a sullen silence.

Soon after that E. L. Robbins arrived with his vacuum cleaner, and while he was initiating me into its mysteries I poured out my grievances as one does into the first ear that comes along. He was all sympathy, and we got very matey over a cup of tea. We had just got to the stage when he was begging me to call him Ernest when Mr Parrish rang down for more breakfast. I rushed round, throwing eggs and bacon into a pan, and roping Ernest in to watch the toast.

'Two breakfasts, upon my word!' he said, scraping the black part off a bit he had burnt.

'Here, put this milk in that little saucepan and heat it up,' I said. 'This wretched egg's gone and broken, but it'll have to do.' It was soon ready, and I clattered off upstairs with the tray, leaving Ernest washing saucepans quite happily in the sink wearing one of my aprons.

My employer was talking on the telephone as I forced my way through the thickness of the atmosphere to his bedside. 'Just going to have some breakfast – is it really eleven o'clock? Yes, I'm still in bed. Isn't it *monstrous*? I know, but I did a lot of work yesterday, and I don't think I feel in the mood to do any more for a bit. All right about tonight? About a quarter to eight, then? Delightful. Goodbye, Simon.' He rang off and said to me:

'You might bring me my letters up here as my secretary isn't coming today. I'll read them in bed.'

I was afraid he might have the idea of using me as a secretary, so I flung them at him and ran downstairs before he could think of it. Ernest had finished the saucepans and was making himself quite at home with the paper and a cigarette. But I had a lot of work to do, so I told him that he'd have to go.

'Anyway,' I said, 'why aren't you doing your own trade? Is there a slump in the vacuum cleaner trade?'

'There's not a lot doing today, as a matter of fact,' replied Ernest, picking up his bowler hat and little attaché-case. 'When can I see you again, my dear? I always love a chat. In any case I ought to bring another screw for that handle sometime.'

I had thought of asking Isobel to come to tea as my employer would be out, so I told him he could come along too, if he wanted to meet an attractive girl. He jumped at it.

'I say, I am a lucky fellow – two ladies all to myself.' I hustled him off down the passage, and he was just going out of the back door, still chattering about 'charming ladies' and 'the cup that cheers', when we suddenly realized that my employer had not signed the agreement which he had brought with him. I took it up to the bedroom, with a pen and ink, but Mr Parrish was lying back on the pillows, looking rather wan, and he waved me away with a limp hand.

'No, no, I can't possibly sign anything today; my

head's terrible. Even to see the printed word – take it away.' I raised my eyebrows and removed myself with the breakfast tray, which showed every sign of having been attacked with hearty appetite.

I explained the situation to Ernest and we did a bit of shoulder shrugging and exchanging of 'Well I nevers', and at last I got rid of him and returned to my house-work. I lugged the 'Sucka' up to the dining-room, plugged it in, and had been having a happy time with it for about ten minutes when a fat figure appeared in the doorway, propping itself up with one hand and holding its head with the other.

'For God's sake stop that filthy row,' he wailed. 'I've been shouting for ages and my head's splitting.'

'I'm so sorry, sir. Very thoughtless of me.' Perhaps he really had got a headache after all. 'Shall I make you a nice cup of tea?'

'God, no!' He retired and I went down, trailing the tube of the vacuum cleaner bumpety-bump down the stairs behind me. It got caught round the post of the banisters when I turned the corner at the bottom and brought me up with a jerk. When I disentangled it I discovered that a rather vital-looking part had been broken off. More work for E. L. Robbins. The edges of the stairs were looking a little dirty so I decided to 'take a brush to them' as I couldn't use the 'Sucka'. There is quite soothing rhythm about brushing stairs, crawling methodically from one to the next, and my brain was lulled into vacancy by the mechanical strokes of my right arm, so that I didn't notice the 'knock, knock, crash, crash' that accompanied the cleaning of each stair. I was soon shocked out of my coma, however, for when I was about half-way Martin shot out of his bedroom with an agonized roar. I gave up. I had done half the stairs anyway. Or, no, I hadn't even achieved that – I had made the elementary mistake of starting at the bottom instead of the top, and had been carefully brushing the dirt down on to the clean stair below.

Martin revived about lunch time and actually managed to stagger as far as the dining-room, where he sat staring moodily into space while I handed him his lunch. I had not reckoned on him being able to eat half a pound of steak and two apple dumplings, so there was not much left for me to eat. I counted up the eggs in the larder, and leaving enough for the omelette for dinner, I could spare myself a couple for lunch.

I put them in the oven to bake while I was serving my employer and, forgetting about them, recollected them just in time to remove them before they should be spoiled. I hurriedly seized a too thin cloth, and, plucking the pots out of the oven, burnt my hands so badly that I dropped them upside down on to the floor. I could have cried with rage and frustrated hunger. Mr Parrish, hearing the crash on his way upstairs from the dining-room, poked his head round the door and said, 'What's broken?'

I hastily put my body between him and the wreckage and said:

'Oh, nothing at all, sir, I just dropped one of the oven shelves.'

I found Mimi in the dining-room, so I hauled her into the kitchen to lick up the eggs. I myself made a pathetic and inadequate meal of bread and cooking cheese. I didn't dare eat any of the fruit in the dining-room, as Mr Parrish sometimes 'fancied' an apple or an orange last thing at night, and, if he ate fruit at dinner, there might not be any left.

He went out quite soon, and I washed up and tidied the kitchen for my tea party. Isobel fell down the area steps and broke a milk bottle, and not knowing that the house was empty was scared that my employer would come out and find her, so I found her hiding in the coal cellar till the danger was past.

Ernest Robbins arrived soon after and I hit on the brilliant idea of making them help me clean the silver.

When it was done, we had tea with masses of hot buttered toast and the best raspberry jam, which Isobel had delved into before I could stop her. I would have to think up a good excuse for its disappearance.

We had great difficulty in getting rid of Ernest. He was one of those people who can never find their way out. I wanted to show Isobel over the house before they came back, but we didn't fancy having him trailing us about through the bedrooms.

It turned out that he had forgotten the screw, anyway, so he would have to come back the next day. Could he be doing it on purpose? I eventually turned him out, saying that I was going to scrub the kitchen floor, and he left us with a:

'Good night all. Thanks for ever such an enjoyable time.'

We toured the house after that, and Isobel was suitably repulsed by the personal habits of my employer. We saw Mr Parrish from the window paddling down the street in a green pork-pie hat, so we had time to rush back to the kitchen before he got in. He came down to get a flower vase. I hastily put away the raspberry jam pot, but didn't bother about Isobel. I didn't think it would matter having a friend in, but it was a bit awkward to know whether or not to introduce them. Mr Parrish evidently didn't expect it, because he stopped on the threshold, said 'I *beg* your pardon' rather coldly and retreated. I shot out and got his vase out of the cupboard for him, saying, for form's sake:

'I hope you don't mind my having a friend in the kitchen, sir?'

'No, but don't overdo it – and *not* men. No followers.'

Isobel made an apt but rather coarse remark as he retired to his bedroom to change. When she had gone I started to cook the dinner. While I was getting the eggs from the larder they 'slipped out of me 'and' and all but two were broken. That wouldn't be enough for the omelette, so, cursing, I had to put on my coat and run out into the rain to the little dairy down the road. When I got back the red arrow was dancing madly in all the spaces at once.

'Wherever have you been?' said Mr Parrish when I rushed upstairs. 'I've been ringing all the bells for ages, I thought perhaps they didn't work.' I had to explain about the broken eggs, and he made no offer to refund me, but I suppose that was really quite fair. 'Will you put out the sherry and tell Mr Nichols to wait in here if he comes before I'm ready? I'm going out now; you might take Mimi for a little run some time.'

'Very well, sir.' (I don't think!) Simon Nichols arrived while I was in the middle of a delicate operation with a sauce, which rather prejudiced me against him. However, he seemed quite a little gentleman, and he and Martin Parrish had a cosy dinner by candlelight, and if I was a little surprised by some of the conversation which I heard when I listened outside the dining-room door I thought no more of it when they had retired to the pink-shaded light of the drawing-room. Tomorrow was pay-day, anyway, so I flung myself with heart and soul at the unin-spiring array of greasy plates and other sordid articles that make up the background of a kitchen life.

Chapter Five

When I had been with Mr Parrish about ten days I began to think it was time I got some pay. I had not liked to ask for my six shillings again, and he seemed to have forgotten about it. I hoped he wasn't going to forget my wages too. I was wondering how I could tactfully jog his memory when he gave me the opportunity himself.

He rang for me one morning, when I was very busy making cakes, to say:

'Will you pay the laundry when they come, for last week, and let me know how much it is?'

I saw my chance to drop a hint. 'I'm so sorry, sir, but I'm afraid I haven't enough money on me. I'm rather short as it's the end of the week.'

'Good Lord, is it? I must give you your wages. I don't owe you anything else, do I?'

'Well, sir, there *was* that money I spent at Woolworth's.'

'What was that? Oh, yes, I remember. Five shillings, wasn't it? Didn't I give it to you?'

'Not yet, sir – it – er, was six shillings.'

'Well, I'll give you ten shillings extra – you can take it out of that when you've paid the laundry.'

He handed me two pound notes, and I went back to take the by now very rock-like cakes out of the oven.

When the laundry man came he was in rather a bad temper as it was raining, and he felt cold and wet and wanted his tea. He looked even blacker when I offered him a pound, and muttered: 'Haven't got any change.' I didn't know what to do, but luckily just at that moment I saw Ernest Robbins' boots descending the area steps. I never thought I should be so pleased to see him. It was evidently his pay-day too, for he was able to supply all the silver we needed. I was sorry to see that the laundry bill came to six and sixpence, so I should have to launch a fresh attack on Mr Parrish's pocket, which always seemed so short of change. I offered the laundry man a cup of tea to cheer him up, but he refused with a mumbled:

'Thanks – no time,' and drove off through the rain.

Ernest said he had come to fit a screw to the handle of the 'Sucka', and I had to give him a cup of tea and some of my burned cakes. I got rid of him quite early by telling him that I 'wasn't allowed followers', in the kitchen.

'Well, it's the last thing in the world I want, my dear, to get you into trouble,' he said, and paddled off quite tractably; I hoped the soles of his boots weren't too thin.

Soon after Mr Parrish and I 'had words'. He came

down to the kitchen with the grocer's book in his hand and a look of dismay on his pink face. I didn't hear him descending the stairs as he was wearing slippers, and he very nearly caught me having a quick swig of the cooking wine which I was using to make a sauce. Trusting that he might attribute my guilty flush to the heat of the stove, I listened in silence while he ranted at me.

'Monica, this is a terrible grocer's bill! I'd no idea you were ordering such strings of things. I really can't have you running up such bills as this, it's absolutely scandalous. Two bottles of salad oil in one week, and all this butter. It's absurd. Either you're very extravagant or they're swindling us. Let me see the invoices. I suppose you've kept them?' This was rather a ghastly moment as, of course, I had never bothered to keep those grubby little lists which bore such mystic signs as 2 Dem and ½ Dig. Bisc. My stomach sank with the cold sick feeling that I hadn't felt since my school days, when one thought the world had come to an end if one was caught talking in the cloak-room.

I hung my head and mumbled.

'Well, really,' said my master, outraged, 'you are impossible – you must do better than that.' I suddenly saw red and all my Bolshie instincts rose and bade me stand up for myself.

'I'm sorry about the invoices, but as to the amount of things on the bill, I ordered what was necessary for the dishes that you asked me to do. I can't cook with air, and the store cupboard was practically empty when I came. Perhaps you would find it more satisfactory to go out and order the things yourself.'

'That will do, Monica. There is no need to speak in that impertinent way. I will think about it, though it is a pity that I should be bothered with household details when I'm so busy.'

I managed to change my involuntary snort of derision into a cough, and Mr Parrish removed himself sulkily.

His aunt came to dinner that night, so I listened outside the door in order to make sure of entering in the middle of a conversation about me, so that I could have the pleasure of hearing them break off suddenly as I went in.

Mr Parrish's French wasn't very good, but he achieved the general idea with:

'*Pas avant le Qweeseenyayer*' as I took in the sweet course.

When I had gone out again, I stamped my feet with a *diminuendo* effect so as to sound as if I was returning to the kitchen, while I really waited outside the door, balancing the tray of meat plates and vegetable dishes on my hip.

The aunt was quite a nice old thing and I'm sure was bored, as everyone is, by the discussion of other people's domestic worries. However, I heard her say politely: 'But she really seems quite a good cook; the dinner is very nice, I'm sure.' (It had been one of my flash-in-the-pan successful evenings.)

'Oh, she occasionally produces things that are quite eatable,' said Martin Parrish in a tired voice, 'but she's a rotten servant really. No experience at all I should think, and a bit of a slut.' There was a pause while knives and forks clattered a little. Then the aunt said: 'I thought she seemed rather a nice-looking girl – quite pretty in a common way.'

'Oh, d'you think so?' said her nephew. '*I* don't.'

Crash! You would not have thought that one gravy tureen lid, sliding to the floor under stress of emotion, could have made so much noise. I went quickly to the kitchen and exchanged my tray for the dessert plates which I took in at once, so that when Mr Parrish said: 'What was that? Something broken?' I was able to say:

'No, sir, one of the fruit plates just slipped out of my hand as I was bringing them in.'

I did not dare add to my unpopularity by admitting the breakage, so my life after this was an incessant struggle to conceal the fact that one of the tureens was minus a lid. Luckily it belonged to a set still in stock at a big store, so I ordered another, but they were very slow in sending it. I had to steer him away from the idea of ordering dishes that needed both sauce and gravy, or else suggest a cold sauce, that would not arouse comment if brought in uncovered.

He told me what he had decided about the bills.

'I don't like to run up these big bills. You are to pay the grocer and greengrocer at the door every day when they come for orders, for what we have had the day before. Be sure to keep the invoices and check them when the things are delivered. Then you can ask me for the money for what we have had before the man comes.'

I thought this was a ghastly idea, and one calculated to give the greatest possible amount of trouble to myself, but perhaps that was the intention.

It turned out to be even worse in practice. I have always been very incompetent about money, and hate having to deal with other people's. What with invoices finding their way into the dustbin, or arriving on a rainy day, an illegible blur, I got into distressing muddles, and was consequently often out of pocket, through having to make good the results of my inefficiency. The question of change was very tedious, too. Mr Parrish never had any, and would give me a ten-shilling note the evening before to pay the grocer, who, after much fumbling in an ancient red leather purse concealed beneath several layers of coats and aprons, would produce one paltry sixpence. I had to toil upstairs to see whether perhaps he had some change this morning, which was rare. I generally had to pay out of my own money in the hope of refunding myself when, if ever, I got change for the note.

One gets used to anything in time, however; even

money worries become part of the routine of the day, and I began to settle down like a fairly contented vegetable into my Campden Hill life.

The thing that was really the greatest bore was E. L. Robbins' pertinacity. The vacuum cleaner was always giving trouble. It would work marvellously for a little, to make me realize what an indispensable joy it was, and would then suddenly develop some extraordinary disease. One terrifying day it started to give off blue smoke and sparks, and other times it would just go sullen and refuse to travel over the carpet in that effort-less glide described in the advertisements. I had, therefore, to send for Ernest, and I firmly believe that, although he mended the immediate damage, he nobbled it in some mysterious way so that he would have to be called in to repair it again.

He was quite useful at doing odd jobs in the kitchen, but it was a bit of a bore to be incessantly making tea, and fobbing him off when he said:

'What do you do on your evenings out?' I wouldn't have minded 'sixpenn'rth of Dark' with the greengrocer, but Ernest did not appeal.

In any case my evenings out were generally devoted to sleeping. Sometimes, when Mr Parrish went out to dinner, I got off quite early, but he was a lazy brute, and generally preferred to dine *chez lui*, often in the company of Simon Nichols.

Christmas time approached and I wondered if he was going to have parties and be very gay at the expense of the poor cook-general. Great was my relief when he announced that he was going to spend it in the country, with Simon and his mother. I heard them discussing it at lunch one day. Kenneth sat silently crumbling bits of bread or poking his food round the plate with a fork. He wasn't going away. I wondered if he had a nice home, perhaps his mother was a callous sort of woman who didn't understand his sensitive little nature. However, I couldn't make out how anyone could be less than over-joyed by the idea of London being rid of Martin for a few days; I myself was almost skipping round the table with the spinach at the thought.

It was one of the spotty girl's days to arrive with her paper parcel, and, still imbued with the Spirit of Xmas Cheer, I submitted quite happily to being told to walk with a piece of satin wound tightly round my nether limbs to test the practicability of the hobble skirt. As I detached myself from the clutch of Kenneth, into whose arms I had fallen after tripping over a footstool, I saw his expression change from a gentle concern to bitter resent-ment. Turning to follow his gaze, I saw that Mr Parrish had evidently answered the door to Simon while we were pre-occupied, and he was now entering the room in a beautiful smooth grey suit. Work was abandoned while he and Martin fell to discussing Christmas plans, and when I took up the tea, spotty face had gone, and Kenneth too. Mr Parrish was going away directly after lunch on Christmas Eve. I was telling Isobel this one afternoon when she was visiting me below stairs, and we were suddenly struck with the most perfect idea.

'Let's give a cocktail party on Christmas Eve, here in the kitchen!'

'Marvellous! It'll be frightfully original – I should think we could cram in at least twenty people, wouldn't you?'

We got down to plans and fixed it all up. Unfortunately, it happened to be one of the days when Ernest Robbins was sitting in a corner of the kitchen, doing something mysterious to the internals of my vacuum cleaner, so, as he had heard all the plan-making, we had to ask him to come. I was glad we did, because he was so frightfully pleased and excited. We told him to come about an hour later than we were going to ask the others, as he was sure to turn up much too early.

About this time, the tradesmen began to get very obliging, in the hope, I suppose, that the master of the house would give Christmas boxes accordingly.

'Some hope –' I thought, but he did actually ask me which ones I thought ought to have tips, so I put in a good word for my special friends. I had discovered a latent charm in the baker, who, at first sight, had seemed uninteresting and stodgy as his dough. This must have been shyness, because, after we had met every day for quite a long time, he quite thawed, and we were soon telling each other our life histories with true back-door lack of reticence. It appeared that he had a daughter – 'Just about your age, our Violet would be. Proper little piece she is, and no mistake. And smart! Keeps the boys guessing all right. She's got a regular now though, lovely steady boy he is – got a good job in the gent's hose at Gamidges. He give our Vi a ring too, straight he did – though of course they'll be walking out for a coupla years or so yet.'

I managed to see that he got something, and also the greengrocer, and the decrepit old grocer. I got my own back on the milkman by telling Mr Parrish that the Milkmen's Union didn't allow Christmas boxes. I hated that man, he looked capable of watering the milk with the tears of little children.

The day before Christmas Eve there arose the important and exciting question of whether my employer was going to romp out with any sort of a present for me. Like the tradesmen, I became almost maddeningly obliging all day, and kept offering nice cups of tea. I even did most of his packing for him, and made doubly sure of not being overlooked, by arriving next morning with a box of chocolates bearing a label saying 'A Merry Xmas from Monica'. He came up to scratch nobly, I must say, and presented me with ten shillings. I was surprised into a last-minute affection for him, as he drove off in his little cream-coloured coupé, with Mimi in her basket on the back seat. Kenneth and I waved from the front door like a couple of old family retainers. He had to stay for a little to write a few letters, but I thought he would be gone by the time I started preparing for my party. I had made most of the food, and was just going to go out to a shop nearby to get the drink, when it occurred to me that I hadn't heard him leave. I looked into the drawing-room, and there he sat by the dying fire, with a writing-pad on his lap and a pen idle in his hand, staring into space. I went up to him, and saw that his eyes were filled with tears, and when I asked him what the matter was, he could hardly speak.

'I'm a fool, I know,' he gulped, 'but it's the ingratitude of it that I can't bear, the awful ingratitude –' To my dismay he suddenly burst into floods of tears, and, though I hadn't the least idea what he was talking about, it was all so tragic that I started to cry myself, and we sobbed on each other's shoulder for fully five minutes. It was a lovely cry, just as good as seeing a pathetic film at the cinema, and when we had finished I think he felt better.

I thought it might cheer him up to tell him about the cocktail party. I made him swear not to tell Parrish and asked him if he'd like to come. He was quite delighted at the idea, like a child, and we went off together to buy the drink. When we got back, Isobel was already sitting on the area steps waiting to be let in. I explained away Kenneth to her when he was upstairs getting something, and then he came down and helped us make the cocktails. He must have had a very weak head, poor darling, for, even after only doing a little tasting, he got wildly excited and started to enjoy himself very much. We explained to him that the party hadn't begun yet, and he calmed down a little, but I thought he was going to become rather a handful before long. Needless to say, E. L. Robbins arrived much too early in spite of our precautions. If we had told him the right time, I believe he would have come before tea. He came in shuffling his feet and holding his hands behind his back, and eventually, giggling coyly, he said: 'Please don't think me a presumptuous chap, but I would like to present the two charming ladies with a little token of seasonable good wishes.'

Thereupon he produced from behind his back two of the most ghastly brooches ever seen on the counter of any multiple store, and, thanking him gushingly, we simply had to wear them.

People were now starting to arrive. We had said 'area steps' on the invitation, and it was funny to see them being amused by what was my daily trek to and from duty. We got Ernest off with an accommodating girl, and the party really went marvellously – that kitchen has never known such a cheerful atmosphere before or since. I had put away most of the crockery, but half-way through the party, Kenneth suddenly fell to the ground like a dead thing, and lay fast asleep with his head pillowed on the remnants of a vegetable dish that he had broken in his fall. We left him there, and he looked so happy and peaceful.

I felt more than disinclined to go back to work on the day after Boxing Day, when I had to go and prepare the house for my employer's return. He was due to arrive at about seven o'clock, so I trailed along as late as possible, and then had a terrific rush to get things tidied up in time. I hadn't felt like clearing up after the cocktail party, and the kitchen looked a wreck. More things had been broken than I had thought, and the electric light bowl was soon pretty well crammed with pieces of china and glass, as well as the cigarette ends and odd bits of food that had been strewn everywhere in drab confusion.

I made a list of the things I would have to replace, and was thankful that I had been given some money at Christmas, though it seemed rather a pathetic way to spend it.

Suddenly remembering that I had not yet lit the drawing-room fire, I rushed upstairs, cleared the grate and laid it in a haphazard way, and did my usual incendiary trick with the methylated spirits. I shook up the cushions a bit to make the room look a little less neglected, and went down to finish the washing up.

I forgot all about the fire, though I had meant to go up and put more coal on it as it burned through, and when I eventually did remember, it was practically out. There was no more methylated, so I resorted feverishly to all the dodges I had ever read of in the *Home Magazine* – lumps of sugar, candle-ends, etc., but all to no purpose. I held a large sheet of newspaper in front of it for ages, and was rewarded at last by a faint crackling. There was more smoke than fire, however, and Martin Parrish had to choose this inconvenient moment to arrive, tired and cross from a long cold drive. He walked into the room where I was still kneeling, and was greeted by clouds of belching black smoke. Coughing and wiping my eyes, I apologized, but he took himself off in high dudgeon to huddle over his electric fire upstairs. When the fire had exhausted itself by smoking, it quietly died. The only thing to be done was to start all over again from rock-bottom, which I did, very harassed by the fact that Mr Parrish called down that he would like to have supper as soon as possible.

When the fire was at last beginning to burn, I hastily laid the table with what was left of the crockery and glass, and heated up a stew of rather dubious age, which had been congealing in the larder over Christmas. I put in a lot of herbs and seasoning, to disguise any possible rank taste, and he ate it all right, but gloomily.

I wasn't going to offer to unpack, in case he accepted, and he luckily didn't think of asking me, so I finished up downstairs quickly, and left him crouched over the struggling fire.

The next high spot was New Year's Eve, and, to my intense disgust, Martin Parrish started to talk about giving a party. He and I made out an approximate list of the food and drink that would be needed, and he took it away to count up the cost. Evidently he found the total too vast, for the next thing I heard was that his ideas had descended with a rush from having twenty people and giving them champagne, to three couples and Simon and giving them bridge and fruit punch. The dinner was to be on quite a large scale, however, and I took the first opportunity of rushing out when I should have been polishing the silver, to replace the breakages of my party.

Mr Parrish was nosing around in the kitchen when I got back, so I had to hide my parcels in the coal cellar until he had gone. 'Where have you been?' he inquired, as I entered humming innocently. He had evidently forgotten that he had told me I could go out any afternoon I liked, I suppose because I hardly ever did, as there was always too much to do.

'Just popped out to get some eggs, sir.'

'Eggs, what for? They're dear just now, aren't they?'

'Well, sir, I – er – thought I might make the trifle today for tomorrow's dinner.'

'Oh, I see, well, I suppose that's all right. We seem to be rather short of glasses. You didn't tell me you'd broken any –'

'Oh, I haven't, sir, I just put some in another cupboard, that's all.'

My prayers that he wouldn't ask 'which cupboard?' were answered, for Mimi started yapping upstairs, so he had to hurry away. The next day was a terrible one for me. I started preparing the dinner quite early, so as not to have such a panic in the evening, and Martin chose that day to have a migraine. He stayed in bed till six o'clock and kept his finger almost permanently on the bell-push all day – I wonder the red arrow didn't drop off. First his breakfast egg was too hard and he must have another, then he wanted some cigarettes, then orange juice, and once it was for me to go into the street and send away a barrel organ. I didn't like to do this without giving the man any money, and as none was forthcoming from the Parrish purse, and I had none, I had to borrow it from Ernest Robbins, who needless to say was in the kitchen again, getting underfoot and altogether being a nuisance.

When Kenneth arrived, he was very annoyed in his gentle way that he hadn't been told he would not be wanted. He had to go up to his employer's bedroom to ask him to sign something, though even that would probably be too great a strain for Martin. I was giving the dining-room a quick flick-over, and I heard a great deal of complaining talk going on – I couldn't hear what they were saying, even when I stood outside the door and polished the knob, till Martin's voice suddenly rose to a scream:

'Damn it all, I pay you, don't I? What else do you want, you jealous little – !' I recoiled and Kenneth staggered out, white and shaking and, before I could try to comfort him, ran unsteadily downstairs and banged out of the front door.

I didn't give Martin much of a lunch, I was too busy doing things for the dinner, but he polished off what I took him quite happily, and then settled down to a well-earned sleep.

As the evening drew on, I was involved in a frenzy of cooking, and getting more exhausted and harassed every minute as I kept remembering things that still had to be done. Mr Parrish did not help my confusion by strolling languidly down to the kitchen with a book on how to make punch, with which he wanted me to help him. I said:

'I can't spare you a minute, sir.'

He was very affronted, and I had to scare him away by nearly spilling some egg on his sleeve as he pored over the book on the table which I wanted to use. I couldn't help it if he was annoyed; he'd be much more so if the dinner wasn't ready, and I did not see why he shouldn't do a little work for his silly party. He shuffled away into the dining-room and spent a sulky half-hour throwing fruit peel, spices, and the contents of various bottles into a huge china bowl.

I got hotter and hotter as I basted meat and stirred sauces like mad, trying at the same time to fry potatoes in a deep pan of fat, which spat viciously at me whenever I went near it. When the door bell rang I was in too much of a turmoil to tidy myself or even take off my apron. My one idea was to rush upstairs and down again to my cooking as quickly as possible. I thought the couple that I admitted looked at me a little queerly, so when I returned below I took a look in the pathetic little square of spotted mirror that hung behind the kitchen door. I certainly was rather a terrifying sight. The steam and heat had turned my hair from a mass of fascinating curls to a sort of hayrick of lank straight locks; spots of brown grease were spattered all over my face, and there was egg in one eyebrow. It was not surprising that the guests had seemed a little taken aback; I looked as if I had some sort of plague. There was no time for repairs now, as a piece of paper, which was covering something on the stove, suddenly caught fire, and dropped black ash into the Hollandaise Sauce. I skimmed and strained it feverishly, but it was useless to try to remove all the little black specks, and equally useless to start it again, as there simply wasn't time. I was in a panic, but I suddenly had a brainwave and turned the sauce into Béarnaise by adding some chopped herbs and gherkins which effectively mingled with the black specks and camouflaged them.

I had barely time to do this before the bell rang again. I hastily did something about my plague-ridden face, broke a comb on my hair, and tied it back with a bit of ribbon. I tore off my apron as I ran upstairs, flinging it into the gent's toilet as I passed. The rest of the party had all arrived together, and I announced them in my most up-stage manner, hoping that the first couple would think that there were two maids, and not connect me with the apparition who had let them in. Dinner was rather a sticky affair, the punch didn't seem to imbue any of them with a wild party spirit. My *bête noire*, the chain-smoking American woman, sat on the host's right and blew cigarette smoke into his face in a half-hearted attempt at fascination. He was still sulking, I'm afraid, and sat hunched over the end of the table, throwing out an occasional moaning word or two by way of conversation. A fat gentleman told long and pointless stories which made nobody laugh except himself, and that only a spasmodic wheezing.

However, I could not pay much attention to the social aspect of the party. Serving up and handing a four-course dinner to six people all by oneself is a distinct strain, and I got pretty hectic. It was difficult to preserve an air of calm efficiency in the dining-room, while my nose told me that all was not well in the kitchen. The necessity for concealing the fact that my hands were filthy was troublesome too. When I cook and dish up in a hurry, it is rather a messy process, what with tasting and all, and of course there was no time to wash before taking the food in. I had to slide my hands carefully under the dishes; it's not easy to get the second hand under, and involves clutching the dish to the bosom, but it's better than shoving a grubby unappetizing thumb under the noses of the guests. When they finally went upstairs to play bridge, I felt as if I had been through a battle, and had to 'take five minutes off' before washing up. When I was in the thick of it, they rang for me to take up drinks, which meant taking off my overall and decking myself out once more in my frills.

One of the tables was holding a rather acrimonious post-mortem, and voices were getting shrill. I withdrew thankfully to my kitchen, whose peace was only broken by the occasional gluggle glug of the Frigidaire. It was half past eleven before I had finished, and I was just going to go when they rang for me again. Martin Parrish came out into the hall and told me to make some more punch for them to drink the New Year in. He offered me the book of words, but I thought I would probably make a better one than he without its aid. I put in all the drink I could lay hands on, which wasn't much as Parrish never kept a proper supply of anything, but I poured in the dregs of any bottles I could see, including the cooking brandy. After adding the fruit, I heated the whole thing to boiling-point, poured a big glass out for myself, and took it upstairs for the still slightly querulous company. It was rather a beastly party really – I was glad to be an accessory and not a member of it. When midnight struck, and grating sounds of 'Auld Lang Syne' floated down the staircase, I drank myself a toast in the poisonous Punch: 'A kick in the Pants for all employers.'

New Year's Eve marked the beginning of a down-grade in my spirits. Work and dirt seem to pile up every day, and I got more and more tired. I was always getting desperate and leaving things to be done the next day, and, in spite of the frequent assistance of Ernest, I never seemed to catch up on myself.

Exhaustion made me miserable, and many were the times when the plates in the sink were washed with my tears of self-pity.

One evening as I was sobbing brokenly over a soup tureen, I felt a trembling hand placed round my shoulders. The back door had evidently been left open and Ernest had walked in all unbeknownst. He was very sympathetic and said: 'Come, come, don't take on so,' and 'dry your tears, little woman.' I soon recovered, if only to make him remove his arm, and we had a long chat about Life and its Injustices which ended by his saying:

'Give notice, dear, that's what *I* say. Face it out, now come on, do.'

Really, when I thought about it, it seemed a good idea. As I felt sure of getting another job, I saw no reason why I shouldn't decamp before I got into a complete rut.

I promised Ernest that I would give Mr Parrish a week's notice the next day, but, by the time I arrived the next morning, I was so taken with the idea of leaving that I felt I couldn't even bear to stay a week. Once I had made up my mind to go, I felt I must go at once or bust, and so, nerving myself for the ordeal, I delivered the bombshell to my master. 'Sir,' I said, depositing the breakfast tray on his chest, 'I wish to hand in my notice.'

He shot bolt upright and spilt some coffee on the grubby sheet.

'Well, really, this is a bit thick! Perhaps you will tell me why you don't wish to stay?'

Common civility prevented me from giving several reasons, so I just said:

'I'm afraid I find the work too tiring, there is really too much for one person to do.'

'What rubbish. Anyone with any method would find this a very easy job, with all the consideration I have given you. However, if you're not capable of managing, there is no use in your staying. I thought from the first that your lack of experience would lead to inefficiency.' As I was going anyway, I thought I might as well let him have it, so I raved, in the most ill-bred and childish way for quite five minutes.

'All I can say is,' I finished, 'that you'll never get anyone to do the amount I've been doing. Your ingratitude amazes me – I shall go at once.'

'No, you can't do that,' he said, regarding me with cold and withering distaste. 'You will have to stay a week or at least until I get someone else – that's the legal position.' I flounced out of the room; as I passed the dining-room I savagely wrenched the handle off the door – it had never been mended – and hurled it out of the window. It gave me the utmost satisfaction.

I bided my time, and maintained a brooding silence all day. Mr Parrish thought he had won, so did not mention the matter again, but gave himself some sadistic pleasure by summoning me upstairs countless times when he knew I was busy, and sending back his omelette at lunch, demanding another one less leathery.

At six o'clock he went out to a sherry party, and with a whoop of joy I let out the emotion that had been bubbling in me all day. I had realized that, if I left my last week's wages behind, I was quite within my rights if I walked out. Thinking to heap coals of fire, I left the kitchen tidy, with the breakfast tray laid ready. When I had removed the things that I had had to buy with my own money, the kitchen equipment was greatly depleted. I had a pang of pity for my successor, so I salved my conscience by leaving behind a rather beautiful green egg whisk. Upstairs, I celebrated my Independence Day by drinking a great deal of inferior Parrish sherry, and, thus inspired, I'm ashamed to say I wrote a very rude limerick indeed, and pinned it, with my thirty shillings wages, to Martin Parrish's pillow.

Chapter Six

After my débâcle *chez* Parrish, I did not look for another job at once. A slight rest seemed to be indicated, and I spent quite a contented few days lying in bed late in the mornings and massaging my hands with cold cream, in a despairing effort to get them back to normal. Also, the family were planning a motor trip in Alsace-Lorraine in the near future, partly to see the country and partly to eat the local food. I wasn't going to miss that for anything, and I thought I might learn a great deal about my Art.

The only regret I had about leaving Martin was that I had never said good-bye to E. L. Robbins. I felt really bad about that. He had stood by me through thick and thin, and it was on his advice that I had eventually given notice, and now I had gone and left him flat without a word. I thought the least I could do was to write a letter of thanks and farewell, which was sent to him c/o The 'Sucka' Company. In a few days I got his reply.

MISS MONICA DICKENS

DEAR FRIEND,

Perhaps you will allow me to pen a few words of thanks for yours. I cannot tell you how I shall miss my delightful visits to your kitchen, and to see yourself and the other charming member of the fair sex. Nevertheless, for your sake, I am delighted that you are no longer subjected to the *inconsiderateness* and may I say *unkindness* of the person whose name I will not mention. In conclusion may I take the liberty of wishing you success in the future, and hoping that you will accept these lines in the spirit of sincere kindliness with which I offer them.

> *I remain*
> *Yours faithfully*
> ERNEST L. ROBBINS

By the same post as this touching epistle came a letter from the agency asking me if I would consider taking a job in the country for three weeks, to help out a man who had a sick wife and three children on his hands and no cook. The call of the kitchen was strong, and the family sounded so nice that I rang up the agency there and then and said that I would just have time to fit it in before going away.

They gave me the address – a Major Hampden, living at Yew Green, a village near Wallingford in Berkshire. I had passed through this county and always been attracted by it and wanted to get to know it better. I pictured myself roaming over the Chilterns in the afternoons when I was off duty, not realizing that I would be much too busy washing up the lunch and making cakes for a nursery tea to even poke my nose out of doors. When I rang up Major Hampden, he was so delighted at the idea of getting somebody that he fairly stuttered and stumbled over his words.

'When would you like me to come?' I asked.

'Oh, at once, at once, if you would be so good. We've been at our wits' end with no one to look after the children – my wife's an invalid – and no one to cook. We've been living on s-sausages and rice pudding, which are the only things I can do. We have an old body who comes in every morning – she'll help you with the housework. Oh, dear, it *will* be a relief to have you here – I can't tell you how p-pleased I am.'

It seemed as if I should have my hands full, what with being a nursemaid, cook-general, and housekeeper all at once, but he sounded so perfectly sweet that I promised to go down the next day.

YEW GREEN GROVE

YEW GREEN

NR WALLINGFORD

BERKS

Wednesday

DARLING MUMMY,

Well, here I am, safely installed *chez* Hampden, after an uneventful journey. The old boy met me at the station in an ancient car tied up with string, and drove me here through lovely country. It's quite a primitive village, sitting at the bottom of the Chilterns, and surrounded by vast ploughed fields, with clumps of elms stuck about here and there. The house is what's known as 'rambling', you hit your head in unlikely places, and a draught whistles at you round every corner. But I like it here, I've decided already.

First of all, let me tell you that, much to my surprise, I am not a servant – I am 'one of the family', and they treat me real nice. It was very amusing trying to find out exactly what my status was. I arrived, all humble, like a tweeny with her wicker basket, to be greeted like a most welcome guest, sat down at the table where they were lunching off Bully Beef and oranges, and addressed throughout as 'Miss Dickens'. Gone are the days when I clear one end of the kitchen table to crouch pathetically over the scraps off the dining-room plates.

Old man Hampden is a perfect darling, and behaves as if I were here as a favour instead of in return for wages. He has mild blue eyes, and wears a fawn cardigan, riddled with holes, and short, tight plus fours. I don't know what's wrong with Mrs H. She lives in bed in a sort of summer-house in the garden; it must be freezing. What is it you have that makes you have to be in the open air? R.S.V.P. The children are adorable and consist of one boy of nine and one of six, and a minute thing of three called Jane. They are very independent, which is a good thing, as I've got to look after them, and the two eldest are at school nearly all day. I didn't tell Mr Hampden that I had never looked after children, and didn't know the first thing about them. The children soon discovered it, and were highly amused each time I slipped up in the ritual of bathing them. However, I didn't drown them. Jane is a little touchy about details, and cried for five minutes because I took off her left shoe before the right. I had to run the bath water, so that the fond parents shouldn't hear.

I begged them not to call me 'Miss Dickens', it sounds so fearfully governessy and flat-chested, so I now answer universally to 'Monty'.

Mrs H. comes in for supper, which we have all cosy and homey by the drawing-room fire. She retires quite early into the Arctic night, so I have come up to my room, which is also Arctic. A bit of my window seems to be missing. I shall go to bed when I've finished this, as I have to get up at seven to dress the children, do a bit of dusting and cook the breakfast. Oh, the delights of a simple country life! But definitely like heaven after the Parrish *ménage*.

All my love to everybody,

From your cookie

MONTY

P. S. – Please send my trousers and any thick sweaters you can find. It doesn't seem to matter what I wear, and it's so cold. I wish I hadn't bothered to bring my uniform.

YEW GREEN GROVE
YEW GREEN
WALLINGFORD
Friday

DARLING,

Still here and still the most popular, seem to be the Most Popular girl in the School. Their last cook apparently was half drunkard and half-witted, and the one before that had religious melancholia and cried all the time. Major Hampden says he thinks that was why her gravy was always so watery – ha, ha. So, as I have most of my faculties, I am quite a change, and they don't seem to mind even when I do make a mess of things. After all, how was I to know how to make suet pudding? I've always tried to forget that such things existed. Jane was sick in the hall after eating it, and I had to clear it up.

I am supposed to keep the boiler stoked up – the old gardener lights it – but of course I forgot yesterday and it went out, so nobody could have a bath. I expected to be ticked off, but no. Mrs Hampden just said:

'Oh, well, it's the sort of thing anyone might

do,' and her husband giggled and said, 'Well, no one must mind if I stay dirty then.' I've quite changed my mind about humanity – the so-called servant problem wouldn't exist if everyone was as nice as these people. Mrs Johns, the woman who comes in the morning to 'do', is a perfect scream. She comes from Devonshire, and something in her inside has slipped, I don't know what, or where to, but the doctors say it's a very interesting case. Her husband has Anaemia and has to sit in the kitchen with his feet up. Why? you ask. I'll tell you. I had it all this morning over our elevenses. A year ago, Mr Johns was: 'real nasty with this Anaemia; wastin' 'e was, Lovey, and "Nellie," 'e says, "I'm goin' to get to me bed and stay there." "Not if I knows it," I says, "if you go up they stairs, you woan't come down again, till you come feet first."' I didn't know what that meant, but apparently it's the way you arrive at your own funeral! All among the sherry and seed cake. So Mrs Johns had a marvellous idea. She remembered something that her sister-in-law's cousin had once told her at a whist drive as an infallible cure for Anaemia. You sit with your feet higher than your head, so that all your blood rushes to your head and keeps you going. It doesn't seem to matter if your feet wither and drop off – Mr Johns' haven't, anyway, and he's been like that for six months. His wife says to him: 'if you bring down they feet, Lovey, you woan't last till Spring.' It seems a depressing sort of existence for him.

I have stuffed the broken bit of my window up with paper, but it's terribly cold getting up at crack of dawn. I just leap into about six jerseys and an overall and rush down to the kitchen, which is a bit warmer. This morning I over-slept and there was a fearful panic to get the children up and the breakfast cooked in time for them to bus to school. I dressed them in the kitchen so that I could do everything at the same time, but the water for the poached eggs simply wouldn't boil, and Peter started to scream because he thought his favourite mistress would give him a bad mark if he was late. Really, it is a bit of a strain coping with it all before breakfast, children ought not to be so lively at such uncivilized times of day. Breakfast is fearfully hearty – you wouldn't know me – I have to sing 'The Teddy Bears' Picnic' and have my hair pulled, answer riddles, and wipe egg off chins, while still feeling half asleep and rather sick.

You might write. You haven't answered my question about Mrs Hampden and her summer-house. She is so nice, but she looks awfully sad, and sometimes cries, I think.

Love and kisses from
MONTY

YEW GREEN GROVE
YEW GREEN
WALLINGFORD
Monday

DARLING,

How absolutely *ghastly*. I wonder if you're right.

Love

M.

YEW GREEN GROVE
YEW GREEN
WALLINGFORD
Wednesday

DARLING MUMMY,

Major Hampden had to go out to dinner tonight, so Mrs H. and I took down our back hair over our cocoa, and told each other our life history. You were right about her – it's awful. She said, quite jokingly: 'The ridiculous doctors have given me six months, isn't it absurd?' No wonder she cries.

Today the children's Uncle Conrad came to tea with their grandmother. She is quite a nice old lady in a black sort of way, except that she would call me Miss Dixon, but I'm afraid Uncle Conrad is not at all normal. Mrs Johns had told me beforehand that he was 'not quite the thing', so I was not unduly surprised when he broke into a thin scream on being told to eat up his chocolate biscuit. The children love

him, and see nothing peculiar; it was a sweet sight to
see Jane and him playing on the floor with dolls.

I have had to discover how to make all sorts of
revolting things, like Sago, Spotted Dick,
Blancmange, and Prune Mould, but I suppose it's all
part of one's education.

No more now, as I must go and wash some wee
woolly garments. I mended Major Hampden's
cardigan one day, but I don't think he really liked it;
he is very conservative and missed the old aerated
feeling. I have hardly been out of the house yet,
except to the pillar box – so much for my ideas of
rustic rambles.

Love to all,
MONTY

YEW GREEN GROVE
ETC
Monday

DARLING,

Sorry I haven't written for such ages. but I've been
most fearfully busy, as Mrs Johns has got flu – I have
to do all the housework alone – not that there's
much dirt in the country compared to London. She
arrived the other day with a streaming cold, and
went about the house saying: 'Oh dear, what it is to
be a laaady.' Whether she meant that she was one, or
envied those who were, I don't know. I don't know

either how Mr Johns will manage to nurse her and keep his feet up at the same time. What a life these people have.

Jane has been with me in the kitchen all day, as her mother is not so well. Her idea of help is to cut all the pictures out of Mrs Beeton and put them into the saucepans. I didn't know she had, until I found a highly-coloured Charlotte Russe in my soup tonight. It's funny, but I hardly break anything here, where it wouldn't matter much if I did. Innumerable were the various things that slipped through my nerveless fingers in the Parrish basement.

Major H. says the church roof needs repair, and they must have a bazaar – not here, I hope.

Lots of love
MONTY

YEW GREEN GROVE
ETC
Thursday

DARLING,

I've been here over two weeks now, and it seems more like two days. I shall be awfully sorry to leave them all. Today I said to Jane at lunch: 'Empty your mouth before you speak,' and believe it or not, she calmly spat everything out all over the table. Logical, I suppose, but messy. The vicar's wife called this morning to discuss the bazaar and laughed at me.

She is a very hearty woman with wild red hair. I suppose a pair of trousers worn with a cooking apron and bedroom slippers does look a little odd, but no odder than her hat.

I have told the children all about you, and they are very struck by the idea, and even mention you in their prayers: 'Make Mrs Dickens a good girl.' Do you feel any better yet?

Your loving
MONTY

YEW GREEN GROVE
ETC
Tuesday

DARLING,

Well, I shall be home tomorrow. The train gets in about six, I think. The Austrian Jewess who is replacing me has arrived, and is very pleasant, so they are fixed up all right.

The church bazaar is off, as my poor old Major Hampden can't think of anything at the moment but his wife. Mummy, I can't write about the awful things that may happen to this dear little family – I'll tell you everything tomorrow.

Till then –
Your loving
MONTY

Chapter Seven

I came home from the tour in Alsace more than ever convinced that I knew less than nothing about cooking, but after visiting the kitchens of almost every inn and hotel, I was fired with an enthusiasm to try out some of the marvellous things we had tasted over there. I determined to look for a job before the flat after-holiday feeling descended upon me.

I was rather put off going to the agency, because while I was away they had sprung a horrid shock on me.

They had never asked me for more than the initial shilling that I had paid to be enrolled on their books, and I, with an imbecile simplicity, had imagined that it was the employers only who paid a fee when they engaged a servant, and had never thought of inquiring what they were going to charge me. Judge, therefore, of my horror when a bill followed me out to Alsace, saying: 'To suiting Miss Dickens, on such and such dates,' or words to that effect. The total came to over £2 and I was furious. I reckoned up that in my various positions, I had earned about £20, and here they were asking for more than 10 per cent of it, as well as taking goodness knows how much from my employers. They could take millions from Martin if they liked, but I grudged them anything out of the earnings of my sweated labour. I went about for a bit muttering, 'Dual commission, it's illegal,' but I had to pay it. Anyway, they had been very nice to me and got me jobs for which I really was not qualified. I decided that this time I would chance my luck with advertisement, so after much thought I concocted something very conceited and sent it to a 'situations wanted' column where it looked most imposing:

'Working cook-housekeeper seeks daily post, capable, honest, and refined – excellent English and French cooking. Write Box —'

I got several answers almost at once, but nearly all of them only went to illustrate the fact that some people never read anything properly, or if they do, they ignore what they see. Some wanted a living-in-maid, and a dear old lady wanted me as a sort of nurse-companion – heating up her milk at night was all the cooking I should get there probably – but the third was quite hopeful.

'In reply to your advertisement in the *Daily* —' (it ran) 'I am looking for a temporary cook-general to do the cooking and housework of a very small house. There are just two of us, and it would only be for about a month, as I have engaged somebody else who is not able to come to me till then – if you are not yet suited, please call at the above address any morning before eleven o'clock.

Yours truly,
(MRS) BARBARA RANDALL

I liked the idea of another temporary job – it doesn't give time for the novelty to wear off, and for one to get sick of it, so I fished out the dowdy hat, which was looking even more battered after quite a long sojourn in an ottoman. I arrived at the address in South Kensington to find a builder's board hanging on the area railings, and a sound of hammering in the air. I looked again at the address on the letter, because it didn't look the sort of house that anyone was living in, but this was it all right, so I knocked, as there was only a hole where the bell ought to be. The door was opened by a very pretty and quite young girl, in an overall with her hair tied up in a handkerchief.

'Mrs Randall?' I said, astutely observing the wedding ring on her left hand.

'Yes – that's me.'

'I've come about the post as cook-general.'

'Oh, are you the advertisement in the *Daily* —, I mean, the one who put it in? *Do* come in, I'm afraid the place is in an awful mess, the men promised to have finished yesterday, but of course they're not nearly done, goodness knows when they'll be out of the place.' She led the way, prattling gaily, to what I presumed was going to be the dining-room in the fullness of time, as there was a round mahogany table in the middle of the room. The rest of the space was cluttered up with toppling piles of books – vases, lamps, and even a dirty clothes basket. Sweeping one or two volumes of the Encyclopedia from a chair to the floor, she told me to sit down, and hunted about among the confusion on the table for a cigarette for herself. When she had lit it up, she leant against the mantelpiece and giggled.

'I've never engaged a maid before, you know,' she said with endearing candour, 'so I don't know all the things to say. I do so badly want to move in as soon as we've got things just a tiny bit straight. The workmen are only in the basement – they're doing something mysterious to the foundations, and building a maid's bedroom – that's why I can't have anyone to sleep in yet, you see. I'm sure you'll do marvellously, if you don't mind a bit of a muddle.'

This was swift work, and my professional instincts told me that it was all wrong that I should have been engaged without having a chance to tell her how marvellous I was – Mrs Hampden had given me a reference, saying I was willing, obliging, and a good worker, which sounded more like a cart horse than a cook, but I produced it now and handed it to Mrs Randall. She barely glanced at it, and she seemed to have made up her mind. I believe she would have engaged anybody, one-legged, armless, or deaf and dumb, provided they'd been the first to apply for the job. She was so pleased at the idea of getting someone, and being able to settle down in her little love-nest – she was obviously very newly married, and I thought she was sweet, and would be delightful to work for. She was small, with curly brown hair and huge wide-open eyes that looked at you innocently out of her pretty round face. She didn't look more than twenty, but I thought it preferable to be bossed by someone younger than myself, rather than by an old trout in a flowered kimono.

After showing me the rest of the house, which consisted only of a drawing-room and dining-room on the ground floor, a double bedroom and spare room upstairs, and a bathroom half-way, we descended to the kitchen, stepping over planks and heaps of cement on the way – the kitchen, however, was more or less ready for use, as far as one could see from the litter of shavings, crockery, and pots and pans that was strewn about.

It was done up quite pleasantly in blue and white, with check curtains, there was a clean-looking new sink and gas stove, but, oh horrors! What was this? The old-fashioned range had evidently been removed, and in its place under the mantelpiece, charged with sinister menace, stood – a boiler. Mrs Randall followed my gaze, which was riveted on it in awful fascination, and said cheerfully:

'You won't mind lighting the boiler in the mornings, will you? Actually – I believe it's quite a simple one. My husband will be able to explain all about it to you, anyway.'

I thought it would have to be a pretty intensive explanation to make me understand it. It has always been my contention that no woman ought to have to look after a boiler. They're simply not made that way – it's like overarm bowling.

However, it would be their lookout if the bath-water wasn't hot through my getting confused with dampers, drawers, and what not.

We arranged that I was to come quite early the next day and between us we would try to get the house straightened up so that they could sleep there that night.

'Oh,' said Mrs Randall suddenly, as I was just going out of the front door, 'we haven't settled anything about wages. Would £1 do?'

'Well, er, hm –' I was going to say that it was less than my usual wage, but it occurred to me that they were probably very hard up and had only just been able to afford to marry. Everyone likes to help young love along, so I said: 'Yes, thank you, that's quite all right.' She looked relieved, and I left her, thinking that the small pay would anyway give me an excuse for being even less thorough than usual. I arrived before her the next day, but the workmen had got the back door open – so I went in that way, and was nearly brained by a small plank that came hurtling from the roof into the area. I looked up, furious, and a face with a walrus moustache looked over the parapet and said, 'Wotcha, Blondie!' I flounced into the house, to be treated to a few desultory tooth-suckings as I passed the future servant's bedroom – where four or five men were sitting on the floor drinking tea out of enamel mugs.

'Never speak to strange men' is evidently not a maxim that applies below stairs, for they were very offended when I ignored them, and yelled out, 'Can't yer say "Good morning"?' So I had to yell back from the kitchen, 'Good morning!' to which they replied, 'Oi-oi' on various notes like a male chorus. However, this wasn't the B.B.C., so I vouchsafed no more, and, putting on an overall, attacked the kitchen with morning zest. After I had put all the rubbish into the dustbin, and arranged the plates and dishes on the dresser, it began to look more presentable. All the crockery was dirty, of course, and would have to be washed, but as I couldn't find any soap flakes or powder, I left it for the time being. I decided to hang up some saucepans. Most of the workmen seemed to have disappeared by now. They had gone either on the roof or on strike, but there was a sad, pale youth of about sixteen sitting in the area, chipping stones, so I bearded him and said, 'Could you oblige me with a hammer and some nails?'

'Yes, miss,' he said, getting up and hunting round in a vague way till he found what I wanted. He handed them to me with an ''Ere y'are', and returned sadly to his stones.

I had great fun knocking in nails at every possible point – I love to see saucepans and ladles and things hanging round a kitchen, it gives it a cosy olde worlde look, and Mrs Randall had lovely new matching sets of everything, which it would have been a pity to hide. The noise of my hammering drowned her arrival and she entered with a shriek as she saw me miss the last nail and hit my thumb. I hopped round the room in agony for a bit, and she trotted after in a distressed way, begging to be allowed to have a look. When I eventually uncovered the injury, there was nothing to see at all, which is often the case, but is always disappointing, so we went upstairs, after she had admired my efforts in the kitchen. A van had deposited several more things in the hall since yesterday. They seemed to have had a lot of wedding presents.

I spent the rest of the morning carrying endless loads of books and knick-knacks up to the drawing-room where she arranged them, prattling all the time. Even when I went out of the room, she raised her voice to follow me downstairs, but nevertheless I missed some of her remarks, and she would say 'D'you think so?' as I arrived back, hidden under a pile of books on a sofa cushion.

'Yes, madam,' I panted, or, if that didn't seem to be the right answer, 'I mean, no, madam.'

Eventually, we couldn't get anything more into the drawing-room, which was already beginning to look rather early Victorian, so we stacked a lot of things in the spare room.

'It's rather a pity,' said Mrs Randall, 'because I shan't be able to have my mother to stay till I get rid of some of this rubbish. Really, why *do* some people have such ghastly taste? Look at this vase, just like a dustbin!'

I thought there was an excuse for it, if it was going to help in preventing a mother-in-law from staying with a newly-married couple, but refrained from comment and descended for a fresh load.

At lunch time she sent me out to buy some sausages, which I cooked, and we both ate them at the kitchen table, washed down with huge cups of coffee and more chatter.

I asked her if she was going to arrange with any of the tradesmen to call for orders.

'Oh, goodness,' she said, 'yes, I suppose I ought. There seem to be quite a lot of grocers and things round here. Mother says it's a good thing to change your tradesmen quite often, as they're more likely to try and please you if you're a new customer, but I shan't tell the first lot that, of course.'

She went upstairs proudly, to get her coat, and I

started in on the crockery washing, as I had bought some soap flakes when I got the sausages. She came down in her trousseau fur coat. 'I say, are you washing all the plates and things? That's *marvellous*. I wonder if you could possibly give us dinner here tonight? Just a chop or something? Could you really – oh, that'll be lovely – what shall I get?' I gave her a list of things; and she trotted out, saying, 'Now don't go and do too much and get tired on your first day.'

What a change from Parrish! I prayed that she might never get like that, but a few years of coping with rather frightful domestics like myself might easily sour that sweet good-nature. Who knows, perhaps even Mr Parrish had been a sunny soul at that age, and had treated his cooks as if they were human, but, somehow, I couldn't imagine it. At tea-time the Walrus Moustache came tramping in a very dirty pair of boots into the kitchen which I had just swept.

'Be a love and put the kettle on, so's we can have our tea.' When it was boiling I yelled out to them, and was answered by the usual chorus of 'Oi-oi', and Walrus came along with a grubby-looking billycan. I pointedly spread sheets of newspaper on the floor between him and the stove, and he advanced over them like Queen Elizabeth, saying, 'Pardon me, Duchess.' I wanted to laugh at him, because he really was very funny, but I didn't dare let him see I thought so. I controlled myself while he poured water on to the black tea leaves in the can, and stirred the whole lot round with a screwdriver – which he carried in his breast-pocket in place of a fountain pen. He picked his way delicately back over the newspaper crying, 'Dinnah is served!' turning at the door to give me a very familiar wink. He seemed to be the leading light of the party next door, because I could hear his voice leading the conversation, interrupted occasionally by the sucking noise of tea being drawn through his moustache. The others expressed themselves chiefly in guffaws.

They packed up soon after this, having evidently come to the conclusion that they had drunk enough tea for one day. The idea of knocking off seemed rather to go to their heads, and I heard a lot of ragging and shuffling in the passage, and eventually a very fat man was propelled violently into the kitchen and landed on his back on the floor.

'He's just come to say good night, miss,' said a grinning face appearing in the doorway. I was beginning to understand how school teachers feel when their pupils persecute them, but I said 'Good night' quite politely to the figure on the floor, who, however, thought the whole thing so screamingly funny that he could do nothing but giggle. He scrambled to his feet with a large red hand over his mouth and tottered out, shaking like a jelly.

I was thankful when the last hobnail boot clattered away up the area steps and I was left in peace. I had been thinking how lovely it was that there were no electric bells in the house yet, but I wasn't sure that the workmen were not even more unnerving.

I was looking forward to seeing the second half of the Randalls, and I knew he was due to arrive soon, when I went up to light the drawing-room fire and found her in a different dress with her hair and face carefully done.

When he arrived she took him all over the house to admire her handiwork, and brought him down to the kitchen to be introduced to me. He was rather embarrassed, as most men are when they have to talk to a domestic about anything that doesn't concern household matters, but managed a shy 'How d'you do?' and a handshake. He was tall, with a good-looking if not intelligent face, and together they really looked the sort of couple that makes old family nurses say, 'Don't they make a lovely pair?'

They seemed blissfully happy and enraptured with everything, even the rather dull dinner I gave them, and when I went up to say good night they were sitting hand in hand on the drawing-room sofa – a charming picture.

'Oh, but my husband must explain about the boiler to you before you go,' said Mrs Randall, jumping up and pulling him towards the door. 'You see,' she said as we all went down to the kitchen, 'it's very important for the water to be hot by half past eight for his bath, otherwise it makes him late for work.'

He seemed to know a lot about the boiler in theory, anyway, and I listened to all the talk about opening dampers, and when to make it draw, and when not to, but I didn't take it all in – it seemed so complicated. Surely in these enlightened and lazy days they could be made a bit more foolproof. Though not at all reassured myself, I assured them that I understood perfectly and left them, praying that all might go smoothly in the morning.

My misgivings were more than justified the next day, when the boiler gave me a taste of the vice in its soul. I made a great effort and, getting up early, arrived at the South Kensington house by half past seven. Much to my relief, the chain gang had not yet arrived, so I took the front off the boiler and carefully filled it with paper and wood. It blazed up beautifully, and I thought I would let it burn for a bit before I put on any coke, so I went upstairs to dust the dining-room. When I got back to the kitchen the boiler stared coldly at me and the ashes of the wood and paper lay dead inside.

I started grimly all over again, and added some coke on top before going up to sweep the carpet. I only stayed away a few minutes this time, but even more depressing results awaited me. Nothing had been burnt except the paper, and the carefully stacked wood and coke had just collapsed, and most of it had fallen out on the floor as, of course, I had forgotten to put the front on.

The kitchen clock told me it was getting quite late, and as I was on my knees, feverishly making another effort at laying the boiler, I was startled by shouts of '*Good* morning!' from the doorway. I was much too rattled to answer, so I just waved them away without turning round.

'Hoity-toity!' said a voice which sounded like the Walrus Moustache's, and though he said no more I could feel from the way my spine prickled that he stayed in the doorway watching me pityingly. Eventually he departed roofwards with a snort and never saw the blaze-up that suddenly happened for no reason at all and nearly took off my eyebrows. This time I stayed by the boiler, and fed it, like an invalid, with one lump of coke at a time, only leaving it for a minute to take up the early morning tea. I was absorbed for quite a long time, dropping bits in through the top, and was trying to persuade myself that it was only my imagination that made the small red glow inside seem to be getting even less, when my employer came rushing into the kitchen in his dressing-gown with a blue unshaven chin.

'I say, what's happened? The water's stone cold.'

'I'm terrible sorry, sir. I've had such trouble with this thing.'

'Oh, Lord, let me look. Here, surely you ought to have this little door open, not this one. Look – I haven't got time now – I'll skip my bath this morning. You might heat me some shaving water.' I put the kettle on and abandoned the boiler, which in any case had now definitely given up the ghost, as it was time to start cooking the breakfast.

When I took up the eggs and bacon they had started on their grapefruit and coffee, and she was reading him extracts from her letters while he was trying to get a hasty glance through *The Times*.

'Mother wants to come to dinner tonight, darling. I'm longing for her to see the house now we're actually in it.'

A mumble came from behind the paper: 'Oh, Lord, what a day, everything at once. First the boiler, and then your mother –'

'*What* did you say, Peter?'

'Oh, nothing, darling, nothing, nothing, nothing. I say – poor old Cummins is dead! Stroke on the golf course – who'd have thought it!'

I went out of the room, leaving her still brooding a little. As she kissed him good-bye in the hall I heard her say: 'Darling, you do *want* to have mother to dinner, don't you?'

'Of course, my sweet, if you want her. Good-bye, darling – take care of yourself,' he called as he rushed off in a great hurry. I wondered what his work was that made him behave like a little boy who is afraid of getting a bad mark if he's late for school.

When Mrs Randall had ordered the meals, which

consisted chiefly of her sucking a pencil and saying, 'Um –' and me sucking my teeth and saying nothing, she said:

'It was a pity about the boiler. I wonder if you could light it now – why don't you get one of the workmen to help you? They're sure to know all about it.'

This had already occurred to me and, though I didn't much like the idea, I saw that I should have to resort to it in the end.

The boiler had got to be lit some time, so I screwed up my courage and when the Walrus came padding in to make the first of those frequent brews of tea I said:

'Could you *possibly* help me to light this boiler? I've tried and tried but it's no good and I must get it lit.'

I sat down, as he was not very tall, and I wanted to be able to throw him an appealing upward glance. He regarded me with the confident mockery of a man who has women in his power and tosses them aside like broken dolls.

'I will ask the second footman to attend to it, your ladyship,' he said, and minced off over the newspaper. A few moments later the pale youth popped his head round the door and said:

'Fred says I've got to light yer biler.' I welcomed him with open arms, and he took the lid off the thing and peered gloomily inside.

'Cor, what you bin at?'

'I know, isn't it awful? Can you possibly get it to light, d'you think?'

'Gimme a knob or two of coal, miss, and I'll soon get her going.'

I rushed out to the coal cellar and returned with my arms full, blacking my face and clean overall in my excitement. He stacked the boiler up methodically with paper and wood, and twiddled a few knobs, and when it was filled with a magical crackling he put on the coke.

'Must have a touch of coal to start it off like,' he said, 'then you can put on the coke when she's glowing, see?' I got him to show me what to do with the wretched little doors, once it was going properly, and thanked him warmly. He had missed his tea through it, so I offered him a cup in the kitchen, which he accepted. 'Got a horrible pain,' he confided to me as he sat down, holding his pale face in his hands, 'it's me teeth. Spent ten pounds on 'em last year, but they don't seem to fit yet. Ma says they always play you up for the first five years. Ten pounds I spent, and they're lovely, too; I think they look ever so nice.' He bared them at me in a false and gleaming grin. I thought it terrible that he should have false teeth at his age; but it seemed more a matter of pride than regret with him. 'Ah well,' he said at length, getting wearily up, 'this won't buy the baby new clothes.' He gave the fire a last poke, and shutting everything down on the cheering glow inside, shuffled back to his stone chipping.

Mrs Randall went out quite early, saying she would not be back till after tea, so I prepared to do a little intensive cleaning. Carpenters and packers had left their traces of dust and shavings all over the house, and I thought that I had better do something before the eye of Mrs Randall's mother, which I suspected would be a carping one, descended on it. I attended to all the more obvious things, such as the stairs and linoleum in the hall, and after sweating much and grief to the knees I got the place to look fairly presentable. I was in the bedroom making the bed when I heard a sound that made my blood run cold – it was the tramp of boots descending the stairs, and, before I could stop him, Fred had galloped along the hall and out of the front door. I was sure he had done it on purpose.

There was a heap of rubble on the top landing where he had descended through the trap-door from the roof. A dirty footmark adorned every stair, and my beautifully polished linoleum was a tragedy.

I was furious and told him so the next time I saw him, but that man had no shame, he just giggled and said, 'Aw, come off it, Chloë.' He insisted on calling me that – it seemed to be his idea of a stuck-up name. I was washing some saucepans at the time and, still assured of his irresistible charm, he offered to help me, a suggestion which I didn't think even worthy of an answer. Lunchtime came with its usual tea-brewing nuisance, and I thought I might try to snatch a little peace to eat an egg or two, and read my morning paper, the dear little Servant's Delight. Fred, however, had other ideas – the kitchen window looked out on to a tiny strip of garden at the back of the house, and this was where he had taken up his stand, with the walrus moustache spread out against the window-pane. I moved my chair to the other side of the table so that my back was towards him, but it was impossible to ignore the melancholy strains of 'You're a sweet'eart *hif* there ever was one, it's yew', which banished all hope of peace and quiet.

After lunch I started to prepare one or two things for dinner. Fred had given up on 'You're a sweetheart', and was working in the next room to the accompaniment of 'Ain't she sweet?'; but I was getting used to it, so it didn't bother me so much.

I was feeling quite pleased with life in general, and had made a mayonnaise without curdling it, but a bitter blow was in store for me. I went to the sink to rinse something out and ice-cold water came out of the hot tap. There sat the boiler grinning smugly with the bars of its front door, and saying, 'I told you so.' I gave it a sharp clout with a rolling-pin, but it wasn't really its fault for going out when I had forgotten to make it up all day. I went to look for the young boy, but he was nowhere to be found.

'Gone home wiv toothache,' said Fred with great satisfaction. 'Something I can do for you, Chloë?'

'Well, all right, blast you,' I said. I felt it was rather a climb down, and I had to stay in the kitchen while he relaid and lit the boiler in case his distorted sense of humour led him astray.

'You got a boy, Chloë?' he said when he had finished, getting up from his knees and dusting his hands. 'Yes, thank you,' I replied. 'He's a heavyweight boxer.'

'O.K., dearie, you win,' replied Fred, retreating with a wave of his hand. I recollected my manners and called out, 'Thanks awfully for lighting the boiler!'

'Think nothing of it, Chloë.' I thought I had heard the last of him for that day as it was time for them to knock off, but while I was rolling out some pastry I realized that a little scene was being staged outside the kitchen door for my benefit.

'Je-ames,' I heard in accents of falsetto refinement, 'would you maynd brushing off my coat? Hit's a trayfle creased. Her ladyship is sure to pass a remark about it.'

'Ho, certainly, may lord. What a beautiful fit, if ay may say so!'

They peeped round the door before they left to see the effect on me. I pretended not to have noticed anything, and rolled away like mad, ruining the pastry, as it turned out afterwards, by pressing heavily on it in my efforts to keep from laughing.

I wished I didn't have to be haughty with them, but I saw no other way of coping with their peculiar brand of teasing … I really felt quite shy of them; they were quite a different proposition from some of the tradesmen with whom I had made friends.

Mrs Greene, my mistress's mother, arrived very early, considering she was only supposed to be coming to dinner, before either of the young couple had returned. She was a small stout widow of about fifty, ambitiously but unsuccessfully dressed in a black satin suit, whose short skirt displayed a great deal of plump leg in shiny orange stockings. A too frisky hat was perched at the wrong angle over her busy little black eyes, which swept over me as I let her in, darted all round the hall, and finally returned to me.

'Yes, yes,' she said, tottering into the hall in her tight court shoes. 'You're Monica, I expect, that's right. I've heard all about you.' I wondered how she knew so much already, but I soon discovered that she made it her business in life to know all about everything. She roamed all over the house, peering everywhere in the most inquisitive way, giving vent to an occasional 'Dear, dear!' or 'Well, I don't know', as she trotted briskly from room to room. When I was laying the table in the dining-room I could hear her rummaging about, opening drawers and cupboards in the bedroom next door. Mrs Randall arrived at this point and they greeted each other fondly. Mrs Greene said: 'I think the house looks sweet, darling. There are just one or two suggestions – but that can wait.

I think you ought to try to get Peter to be more careful of his clothes. This suit will have to go to the cleaners; look here, there's a terrible stain on the coat, and the trousers want pressing.'

'Yes, mother. Would you like to come upstairs and have some sherry? I'll ring for Monica to bring some up.'

'Don't ring, dear, she's just in the dining-room, I think. I'll ask her. You look tired, my darling. I hope you haven't been doing too much. Come and put your feet up on the sofa, I'll make you comfy.'

'No, really, mother, I –'

'Come along, dear. Goodness, you get thinner every day. I hope you're eating properly.'

When I took up the sherry Mrs Randall was reclining obediently on the sofa, while her mother pottered about the room, moving ashtrays and ornaments. She seemed to devitalize her daughter and sap her of her usual bubbling personality. But the effect on her son-in-law was even more noticeable. He started off dinner making a great effort at a rather hearty politeness, rubbing his hands and laughing at nothing. Mrs Greene's incessant flow of remarks soon wore him down, however, and he sank into a depressed and glum silence. After dinner Mrs Greene actually had the sauce to come down to the kitchen to see what sort of a hash I was making of things. She arrived just as I was going to have some food, which infuriated me. She was one of those women who don't realize that servants do anything so human or normal as eating, and my supper stood congealing on the table while she talked to me and poked around in the cupboard.

'My daughter doesn't know much about housekeeping yet, you know. I've taught her a lot, of course. I've run a house now for thirty years with no fuss. Do a lot of the cooking myself, too. My daughter always says I give her better food than anybody.' I murmured false sounds of approbation, but could not bring myself to answer when she said: 'I'm surprised to see you using self-raising flour; it's so much better, you know, to use the plain and add baking powder. Still, you're young. You've plenty of time to learn.' Taking my silence for agreement, she left me, to my intense relief, and went away to see what other improvements she could make in the world upstairs.

Chapter Eight

The next morning was catastrophic. I made no attempt to light the boiler when I got there, thinking that I would get False Teeth to do it when he came. The rest of the workmen arrived, and I waited and waited for him, until finally it was getting so late that I had to accost Fred.

'Bert ain't coming 'smorning,' he said. 'What a disappointment, eh, Chloë?'

'You light it,' I said decisively, and remembering the heavyweight boxer, he did. It was too late though, and I was treated to the same vision of Mr Randall in his dressing-gown, saying that the water was an improvement on yesterday, but how the hell was he to have a bath and shave in tepid water? I quailed; he was really angry, probably still the aftermath of the evening before, and he sat down to breakfast, ready to fly off the handle at a moment's notice. His poor tactless little wife remarked brightly from behind the coffee-pot:

'Mother says your brown suit ought to go to the cleaners, darling –'

'Does she, indeed?' He lowered *The Times* and glared at her. 'And what the hell business is it of hers, anyway? If that old witch puts her nose into our affairs any more – I'll kick her out of the front door.'

'Peter!' Mrs Randall clutched the arms of her chair, aghast. 'Darling, how *can* you talk like that about mother? I thought you liked her – you were all over her before we were married.'

'She was all over me before she found out I hadn't any money.'

'What a beastly thing to say – after all the trouble she takes, the things she's done for us.' She was on the verge of tears.

'Well, it's her or me. I warn you, Ba, if she comes messing around here much more – I shall walk out, and you can go back and live with her – you're always telling me how marvellous it was!'

'You beast! I shall, I shall,' she sobbed as he strode out of the room, nearly knocking me down, clapped on his hat, and banged out of the door. I had, of course, been listening in the hall. I wasn't going to miss a good row for anything, though it did distress me to hear two people who really loved each other saying things they didn't mean in the heat of the moment.

I thought I'd better look in and see if she was all right, and she looked so pathetic, weeping brokenly, that I forgot I was only the cook and took her in my arms to try and comfort her; she was much younger than me, anyway. It seemed to be my fate to have people crying all over me. I wondered who it would be next, probably the Walrus. I felt it wasn't exactly what I had been engaged for. 'It's not my work,' I said to myself, patting and making soothing noises automatically. Eventually she came to, and, hiccupping madly, told me All. 'I haven't told him yet, you see,' she said, 'and now I don't see how I can.'

'Well, you are a silly ass,' I said, forgetting my place completely. 'Why on earth didn't you say anything before? You tell him the minute he comes home, whatever you do. You'll be able to have your mother here every day, or anything else you like.'

She cheered up and became more normal, and I remembered that she was my mistress, and apologizing for my loss of respect, I withdrew.

She evidently took my advice for, after this, there were no more rows for a bit, and Mr Randall cherished his wife with an even greater affection than before. She, on her side, continued to only have her mother about the place during the daytime.

However, they were evidently both the sort of people to whom life without an occasional quarrel is a slightly dull and monotonous thing. After three or four evenings of amicable and often amorous conversation at the dinner table she started to goad him, over the steak-and-kidney pie, about one of his friends. They had been talking about giving a house-warming dinner party, and were discussing whom to ask. He said:

'Well, we must have old Godfrey – he's so amusing – make any party go.'

'Oo, darling, *you know* I can't bear him, he's so common and – and *uncouth*.'

'Since when have you been so particular? What about that shocking boy-friend you used to have? Ronald – Donald – Harold, whatever his ghastly name was.'

'That was quite different. He was a gentleman, which is more than you can say for Godfrey. Anyway, I was very fond of Ronnie.'

'My dear Ba, you know you couldn't stand the sight of him. You only took me in order to get away from him.' This was an effort to be conciliatory, but she wasn't having any.

'I wouldn't have done that if I'd known what your friends were like. What you can see in that conceited great ape I simply can't imagine.'

'Shut up, Ba,' said her husband, now beginning to lose his temper. 'I put up with your mother, and you're jolly well going to be agreeable to my friends.' I should have left the room long ago, but, as usual, I was much too intrigued and remained, fiddling with things on the dresser as an excuse for staying, though they didn't really notice I was there.

'Well, I'm going to have mother to the dinner party, anyway.'

'My God, you're not! No, darling, it's no good your throwing your "condition" in my face, because this time it makes no difference. That woman'll bitch up the whole show.'

'Don't call me "Darling", it doesn't ring true. You're the most selfish, inconsiderate, ungrateful beast of a husband I've ever met. I wish you – I wish I never –' Unable to control her tears any longer, she pushed back her chair and rushed into the bedroom with her napkin to her eyes.

'Oh, Lord, these hysterical women,' said her husband, half to himself and half to my back view as I withdrew disapprovingly. We females must stick together, and whether I thought so or not I wanted to convey that he was in the wrong, not that they either of them noticed me when they were heated up about something. It was a curious casual attitude they had towards me, and the world in general for that matter. They were perfectly friendly, so friendly in fact that they behaved with an almost detached lack of reticence, and certainly no feeling of self-consciousness. I suppose it's a sign of these modern times, this breaking of every rule and pretence observed by our grandparents and their forebears in order to keep servants 'in their place'.

This quarrel, of course, was made up as rapidly as it

had started, and there were one or two others of the same calibre before there dawned the day of the First Dinner Party. I was amused to hear that both Godfrey and Mrs Greene were to be among those present, so neither side had achieved anything by the arguments, except a waste of time which they might have spent being happy together.

One other married couple made up the rest of the party, which I did want to be a success for my mistress's sake, and also to show the Greene monstrosity that other people in the world besides her could arrange and cook a dinner.

I took a lot of trouble over it, and spent a very busy day. Fred was even more annoying than usual and did his best to put me off by popping into the kitchen with such questions as, 'Do you know Monica? Monica who?' and rolling round the room convulsed with laughter at the rather rude answer.

I was going to give them a *soufflé* to start with, hoping to time it right, as I had done with my first one at Miss Faulkener's. Mrs Greene arrived first, needless to say, and noticed that the umbrella stand had been moved from one side of the hall to the other. The other couple, a very pretty dark girl with a nondescript husband, arrived soon after, and, when I announced them, I saw her watching them and taking in every detail. I hoped, for their sakes, that their clothes were new or fresh from the cleaners.

I had put the *soufflé* into the oven when Mrs Greene arrived, and I was beginning to get more and more nervous as the minutes passed and Godfrey had not come. It was nearly cooked and, if he didn't come soon, would be completely spoiled. There came the moment when it had just risen to its full height with a billowing brown top and should have been served at once. I turned down the heat, but had to leave it there as there was still no sign of the wretched man, and I began to sympathize with Mrs Randall in her dislike, when a cascade of knocks thundered on the front door and I rushed upstairs. Godfrey was a large panting man with protuberant eyes and teeth, and a distinct tendency to pinch servants' behinds. I whisked mine quickly out of the way, and announced him and dinner at the same time.

I opened the oven door with trepidation and saw that the *soufflé* was rather flat but still fairly presentable. By the time I had carried it upstairs, however, it was flatter than ever, and looked what it was – a failure. I was very upset as I knew my mistress was very nervous and desperately wanted everything to go off well. She would not realize that the *soufflé* was spoiled through waiting and would think I had let her down. There was no hope of her mother not noticing its appearance, as I had to hand it to her first. It was one of the most ghastly moments of my life. Everyone was watching as I produced my poor wizened offering, and I would have given a fortune to have been able to turn it upside down on the closely marcelled head of Mrs Greene, whose gloating smile of superiority as she took the smallest possible helping was the last straw. Mrs Randall looked like a child who has been promised a treat and then disappointed; she opened her eyes very wide at me in mute inquiry. Only Godfrey seemed to take the affair in his stride; he took a large helping without looking at it and proceeded to tuck in, talking with his mouth full to the dark-haired beauty on his right. He was very taken with her, and from her expression of faint loathing and his of suggestive glee he seemed to be saying some pretty impossible things. Her husband was staring glumly across the table and paying hardly any attention to Mrs Greene, who was apparently telling him her life history. My brain took in all this automatically, it was so used to spying on other people's affairs, but I was really too shaken by the catastrophe of the first course to pay much attention to the party. I just got a general impression of ghastliness from Godfrey, which grew as the dinner progressed, and he became more frightful than ever. The only good thing about him was that he prevented Mrs Greene from leading the general conversation. For some inexplicable reason the host found him extremely amusing and roared with laughter at his stories, encouraging him to still further futilities. It was not that his jokes were vulgar, perhaps there would have been more point to them if they had been, but it was a sort of tap-room humour, interlarded with cries of 'Ha-ha-ha! What?' from Godfrey as he invited everybody to join in the fun.

The rest of the food held its own fairly well, though it was not impressive enough to make up for the *soufflé*. The fried potatoes had gone flabby, and I had forgotten to put any jam in the trifle, and little things like that, and I saw Mrs Greene noting every slip. I felt embittered, and thought sourly that they wouldn't have me long, anyway, but Mrs Randall completely disarmed me by running down to the kitchen after the ladies withdrew and saying:

'It was *a lovely* dinner, Monica! Thank you so much for doing it so nicely. I'm sure everyone thought it was marvellous.'

'I'm afraid the *soufflé*, madam –'

'Oh, that didn't matter, it was perfectly all right, really. Mother said you'd timed it wrong, but I suppose it was the fault of that ghastly Godfrey creature. Oh dear, I shouldn't say that, I suppose. Well, good night! Go home as early as you can, you must be tired.' Bless her heart. I really got quite fond of her before my month was up and, in spite of the quarrels, was quite sorry to leave them.

The workmen finished at last, a few days before the new maid was due to come and occupy the bedroom they had constructed for her. I had got so used to being baited that I was even quite sorry to see them go. There was a touching scene when they all filed into the kitchen, outwardly solemn but inwardly giggling at their own drollery, and I said goodbye to each. It was rather like Snow White and the Seven Dwarfs. Like Dopey, Fred came back for more after they had gone and lingered for a few words.

'Y'know, Chloë,' he said, shaking his head, 'you bin a great disappointment to me. Maids is my speciality – when the wife's not around.' I was surprised; I had somehow not imagined him as a married man. I apologized for my lack of response to his charms, and he patted me on the shoulder and went out, saying patronizingly:

'Ah, well, we can't all be hot stuff. I expect you're not ripe for romance, dear, that's what it is.' He gave me another of his winks, well satisfied with his parting shot.

'Why, you –' I cried, picking up the rolling-pin, but he was gone, whistling away down the passage and out of my life. The Randalls and I parted affectionately. He came down to the kitchen before going off to work and, fearfully embarrassed, pressed a pound note into my hand. 'No, really –' I said, deeply touched, but pocketing it before he could take it back. 'I've so enjoyed working for you, sir, you've been ever so good to me.'

More embarrassed than ever, he mumbled his way out of the kitchen door and ran up the stairs, vastly relieved to have got it over. I was more than ever convinced by this time that there are only two types of men in the world – those who are shy of maids and those who are not shy enough. Before we parted I asked Mrs Randall to give me a reference, and she didn't know what to put, so I offered to help her, and between us we concocted the following flight of fancy:

'This is to say that M. Dickens has worked for me for several weeks in the capacity of working cook-housekeeper. I found her sober, honest, and most refined, a very well-spoken girl. Her cooking, both plain and fancy, is excellent; she is scrupulously clean in her methods and her person, and has no eccentricities of religion.'

I had really enjoyed being at the Randalls and thought it would probably be difficult to get anywhere else as pleasant. Not wanting to risk a repetition of the Parrish episode, I turned over in my mind the idea of taking something quite different – perhaps going to the country as a living-in cook and seeing a bit of Servant's Hall life. Though up till now I had thought it preferable to be on my own in the kitchen, it always meant doing housework, and the idea of escaping that particular form of drudgery appealed to me enormously.

I scanned the situations vacant columns to see if there was anything attractive before inserting an advertisement of my own. There seemed to be even more demand for living-in cooks than for 'dailies', and one notice in particular caught my eye. 'First-class Cook wanted immediately for country. Staff 8. Kitchen-maid kept. Own bedroom. 3os. a week. Apply – Housekeeper, Chilford House, Birching, Devon.' Thirty shillings sounded like big money, considering that I would have no opportunity of spending it, so I wrote to the address given and generously offered the housekeeper that paragon of skill and efficiency – myself.

She answered quite soon, telling me to call on a certain day at – (Here followed the address of a flat in a fashionable block.)

I tortured the black hat into an even more uncompromising no-nonsense shape, that added a great deal to my age but nothing to my charms, and set off in a coat that was too long for me and a pair of 'sensible' shoes.

Arriving at the luxurious entrance hall of the block of flats, I felt too humble and unprepossessing to use the lift, so trotted modestly up four flights of stairs and arrived panting at my destination. I was let in by a stout black body of about fifty who I guessed to be the housekeeper, and she led me to a sitting-room, half shrouded in dust-sheets. In spite of the vastness downstairs the flat was quite small, evidently a *pied-à-terre* for occasional visits to London.

We sat down on two of the unshrouded chairs and she began to ask me searching questions with a terrifying intensity of manner that made me more nervous than usual. She was all hung about with emblems of religious fervour; gold crosses on chains, and holy-looking brooches were scattered at random over her person. She jangled like an old monk and this put me off, making me unable to do myself justice, so that I was quite surprised when, after reading my references and even holding them to the light to detect any forgery, she said: 'I'll engage you. The first week shall be in the nature of a trial, you understand, giving me the opportunity to make a change if I'm not satisfied. You wish it to be a permanent job, of course?'

'Oh, yes,' I said, casting down my eyes so as not to have to lie to that penetrating stare. I knew I should not get the job unless I gave the impression that I was prepared to live and die if necessary in the service of Chilford House.

I couldn't really understand why she had engaged me at all. She was the sort of woman you can't fool, and must have sized me up at once for the incompetent and inexperienced messer that I was.

I realized afterwards that she didn't want to have anyone in the kitchen of Chilfor House who might challenge her supremacy over its domestic affairs, which she guarded jealously. She didn't even tell me the name of my future employers or how large a household it was. We arranged such details as half-days, and then she intimated that the interview was at an end, saying:

'It would be convenient for you to arrive tomorrow as

we are making do at the moment with a village woman, but it's *not* satisfactory.' Then she told me the time of the train, and I left her, feeling elated but rather in the dark about the immediate future.

To make myself look more like the country house cook of tradition I bought a whole lot of vast white aprons, which enveloped me starchily and gave me quite a look of ample cosiness. These I packed, with the rest of my things, into a battered suit-case and, dressed once more with a suitable but drab respectability, bade farewell to my family who were by now more than ever convinced that I was crazy.

'You must live in your part, get yourself under the skin of it' had been one of the frequent sayings of the old lady of my dramatic school, so I started in right away. At Paddington I settled myself diffidently into the corner of the carriage and read a twopenny *Home Blitherings,* my face, innocent of make-up, shining like a young moon and my unrouged lips moving with absorbed delight while I followed the lines with my finger.

At Exeter I had to change into a little local train which stopped at every station for the guard to have a gossip, before it eventually arrived at Birching. A porter directed me to a sort of lorry, which looked as if its usual function was to take pigs to market, so I threw my case into the pig part of it and climbed up beside the red-haired youth who lounged in the driver's seat.

'Good afternoon!' I said brightly. 'Turned out nice again!'

He seemed to feel that he was destined for higher things than fetching cooks from the station, for he vouchsafed no more than a mumbled 'G'arternoon' and a sniff. I was determined, however, that in this job I was going to get on with everybody and everything, so, thinking to draw him out by flattery, I asked, 'You the shovver?'

'No!' he roared with scoffing laughter. 'Gardener's boy more like!'

He was tickled to death by my remark, and though obviously disinclined for further conversation, continued to give vent to spasmodic guffaws as we rattled and bumped along the narrow Devonshire lanes, bright with the first green of spring.

Eventually we turned to the left through an open lodge gate and drove up an avenue of oak trees which ran alongside a large park. We came to some iron gates, and I just caught sight of a low grey stone house at the end of a gravel drive before we swung away uphill to the left. We passed a farm and, describing a circle, arrived via the back drive and stables at the kitchen entrance of Chilford House.

'Here yew be,' said the gardener's boy. 'In yew go.'

I got out, heaving my luggage after me, and he drove away at once, leaving me standing forlornly on the gravel with a tin suit-case at my feet.

The door was open so I stepped inside and advanced apprehensively down the dim red-flagged passage to the unknown regions beyond.

Chapter Nine

My first impressions of Chilford House were so confused that it took me one or two days to get everything sorted out, days which passed in a whirling panic of new faces, voices, and masses of food. I thought at first that I was going mad, because there seemed to be more to do than I had ever imagined possible. However, when I stopped being hysterical about the whole thing, and the mists cleared a little, I saw that by systematic concentration I might succeed in saving my reason. My work was only cooking, and though it involved coping with the nursery and kitchen meals as well as the dining-room it made it easier to apply some sort of method. I calmed down after a while and was able to take stock of my situation.

Chilford House was divided into two parts by the green baize swing-door which separated the kitchen regions from the abode of the Gentry. My life, of course, was centred on the inferior side of that door, and indeed I hardly went through it all the time I was there. Although I had nothing to do with 'them' on the other side, they were the subject of so many intimate and derogatory comments in the servants' hall that there was not much I didn't know about them.

My mistress, Lady W—, was a semi-invalid lady of nearly eighty, who had long handed over the reins of government to Mrs Lewis, the housekeeper. She was the mob cap and shawl type of old lady, and spent most of her time sitting in a basket-chair with a high hood back to it, like a Punch and Judy show. I only encountered her after I had been there a week, when I fell off the under-housemaid's bicycle right under the nose of her Daimler as it turned out of the drive on its way to evening church. She had not the slightest idea who I was, but smiled graciously, and, lowering the window, hoped I wasn't hurt. Little did she know that it was I who was responsible for those creamed sweetbreads that she loved, or for that matter one or two little errors such as overdone beef, lumpy sauces, and burnt porridge, about which Mrs Lewis had been instructed to 'speak to me'.

Sir Harold W— was slightly younger than his wife and still quite hale. He ambled about in a tweed jacket with leather patches all over it and a sloppy, slobbering spaniel at his heels. He did himself extremely well, and after the third glass of vintage port had turned him a rare old mulberry colour there would be talk of apoplexy in the servants' hall.

The house at the moment was filled with their children

and grandchildren whom I never got properly sorted out. Their son and two daughters, all married, were staying over Easter with their young in various stages of child-hood, pimply adolescence, or maturity. I caught an occasional glimpse of a young man in a racing car, or a buxom girl pounding up the back drive on a huge grey horse with enormous feet. Various children buzzed into the kitchen at odd times during my first few days and said: 'Where's Mrs Munny? Who d'you think *you* are?' grabbed a cake or anything handy and rushed out again before I could introduce myself.

Much more fascinating than the family was the staff, who were gradually sorting themselves out from a rather terrifying mass of humanity into individuals. Mrs Lewis lived a life apart, suspended as it were permanently in space between the upper and lower regions in a bedroom and sitting-room of her own. She even had her meals carried there on a tray by Nellie, the under-housemaid, and only descended to the kitchen to order the meals and quiz into the larders and store cupboards.

The rest of her life which was not occupied with letter writing and linen cupboards was spent, apparently, in prayer.

'Locks herself in,' Nellie was saying one day as we all sat at the table in the servants' hall over a huge lunch of pork – 'praying away like nobody's business – praying to the devil, I should think – the old cow.'

'Now then, my girl,' this from Dawkes, the butler, 'mind your tongue.'

'You mind your own business,' retorted Nellie, who had no respect at all for the conventions. Besides Dawkes and Lady W—'s personal maid, Miss Biggs, there were two parlour-maids and a head housemaid who all came above her on the social scale. I wasn't quite sure where I came in. For some mysterious reason all cooks, whether married or not, like to be addressed as 'Mrs', and I was universally known as 'Mrs Dixon', which, though it made me feel rather illicit, gave me quite a standing. Dawkes ignored Nellie and offered Miss Biggs another slice of pork. She was a withered old thing, who had grown so grey and wizened in Lady W—'s service that her corsets didn't fit her as well as they used to and made her high-necked dress of lavender silk stick out like a shelf before and behind. Her two pen-chants were for platitudes and food, and she now attacked a tempting piece of crackling with zest, but it proved too much for her ancient teeth and had to be spat genteelly out behind her hand.

There was certainly no stint of food in this house, and I wondered what Lady W— would say if she had any idea of the waste that went on and the innumerable little newspaper parcels that found their way to village homes under the coats of chars, pantry-maids, and even tele-graph boys. Almost every day I cooked a big joint for the kitchen alone, and Dawkes sat at the head of the table and carved it as if he was cutting up bodies.

He had one of those hungry-looking death's-head sort of faces with deep-set eyes, and was a complete dual personality.

On the farther side of the baize door he was apparently the perfect stage butler, and in spite of his rather criminal appearance was highly prized by his employers for his efficiency and loyalty to the family. In the servants' hall, however, though he occasionally, for form's sake, rebuked 'the girls' for an indiscretion, he was a perfect sink of slanderous gossip about the entire family, and anyone else who came to the house. He was a good actor, that man, he even had a special voice which he used when he was being a seneschal – I could hear it sometimes floating through from the dining-room. When he was relating a juicy piece of scandal to us, pop-eyed with eager appreciation, his accents would become the lowest of the low, and his expressions not always suitable for the youthful ear of Polly, the kitchen-maid, who, however, was so simple that she didn't really take it all in. It made me feel very superior to have someone to boss, even such a half-witted creature as she was. She was not much practical use as she would get into a panic if spoken to sharply.

I, being myself in a frenzy to get things done in time, yelled: 'Hurry up with shelling those peas, for heaven's sake!' She would drop everything and rush about wildly with her apron over her head.

'Lor!' she would scream, running round the kitchen in small circles. 'Oh! whatever shall I do? Oh, Mrs Dixon, don't hustle me, I feel ever so queer!'

I wondered why such a mad creature was kept on, but apparently a kitchen-maid's life is such hell that no normal girl will take it on.

She cherished a dog-like passion for the chauffeur, whose name, appropriately enough, was Jim Driver. He had a room over the garage, but being a bachelor took his meals with us, and Polly could hardly eat a thing for staring at him. He was a young man of about thirty whose slight tendency to boils on the back of the neck was counteracted by bright blue eyes and a tinge of Irish in his speech. Apart from the embarrassing Polly, whom he ignored, he distributed his favours impartially among the girls, treating me at first with the deference due to my married name and recent arrival. He had no rival as Dawkes was definitely out of the market. He took no interest in women as such, though he was reputed to have at least two wives secreted in different parts of England.

I think it will give a clearer idea of my life in this intriguing household if I run through the events of one particular day, picking one at random from those that stand out in my memory and starting at the chill bleak hour of seven o'clock when the alarm cut shrilly into my dreams.

I had been at Chilford House about a week, and no longer spent a minute or two of semi-consciousness wondering where I was. My little room, with its sloping attic ceiling that stunned you if you sat upright in bed, was by now quite familiar, but this morning as I travelled my eye round the room from where I lay I reflected that it could never really be made a home from home. I had stuck a lot of photographs about, and even stolen some flowers from the garden after dark, but nothing could disguise the blackness of the iron bed or the yellowness of the chest of drawers and vaguely indecent-looking wash-stand. Old-fashioned, cheap wooden furniture has a peculiar smell, a sort of indefinable mixture of acid and old boots, and I had to sprinkle a great deal of lavender water about. In spite of this I got such a mania about the chest of drawers that I thought it was infecting my clothes, so I kept most of them in the tin suit-case under the bed. Its lock now took a piece of skin off my ankle as I put my feet on to the tatty little red mat, and I hopped painfully over the bare boards to take a look at the day. The view from my window was the chief attraction of my Royal suite. I looked out over a long lawn, cut in three terraces, with a lily pond in the middle, and ending in a ha-ha wall which dropped into the park. I could see a few deer grazing among the scattered oaks, which were the only things that broke my vista of green, until the park ended with a jumble of roofs and a steeple that was the village. 'Very sharp for the time of year,' I said to myself, shivering, in spite of the sun which was picking out the dew with a dancing sparkle. It was too cold to do more than wash my face before putting on one of my vast aprons over a layer of very unglamorous woollen under-wear that was a relic of the Yew Green days. After my usual battle with the mirror – it would swing forwards all the time and present me with its back view – I got my hair and face done – and hurtled down the back stairs to my kitchen. It was warm there, because the huge fire in the range was never allowed to go out; it heated the water and did all the cooking that wasn't done on the gas stove.

Polly was before me and working away like mad. It was her job to clean the kitchen before breakfast. Nellie, who rose early to lay fires, used to see that she got up, and would chivvy her down to the kitchen. Once started off, she could work like a clockwork train, unless somebody threw a spanner into the works by shouting at her and making her panic.

'Hullo, Mrs Dixon,' she said, looking up from her pail and scrubbing-brush on the floor. 'I'd a lovely dream last night.'

'Did you, now?' I said, hurling coal on to the glowing remains of last night's banked-up fire. 'What about?'

'About him – Mr Driver, I mean. 'E come right up to

me and kiss me, ever so gentle, and what do you think he says?'

'Go on, Poll, tell us.'

'"Polly," he says, "you are my dream girl, I love you," he says, just like that – then I come all over faint and sorter melt in his arms. Cor, it was lovely.'

'Then what happened?'

'Well, I wake up then and take a look at me dream book, and it says, "To dream of a kiss from the beloved one is a sign of impending stomach disorder." Still, it was a *lovely* dream.'

She returned to her scrubbing, still wrapped in a reminiscent ecstasy, and I put an enormous kettle on the stove and started to cut bread and butter for the innumerable trays of early morning tea that had to start going upstairs from seven-thirty onwards.

Nellie and Rose, the head housemaid, were responsible for this, and they had a slate which hung in the pantry where the little trays lived on which they wrote down what time everybody had to be called. Rose, who was an unimaginative but conscientious girl with a suet-pudding face, would write the names and times in a laborious script, giving full titles where necessary: 'Major-General Sir Robert W—, Bart, D.S.O., 8.15. The Right Reverend Bishop of Bradshaw, 8.30 – brown bread and butter,' were current entries. The flippant Nellie would add comments underneath, such as 'Sour puss', 'Bald as a coot', or 'Pot-belly'. She said it helped her to remember who was who.

All I had to do was to fill the teapots from the kettle and plank two or three slices of bread and butter on each tray as they brought it in.

Soon after this I started one of my frenzies. Nursery breakfast was at eight-thirty and the dining-room started at a quarter to nine, not to mention a coddled egg and melba toast for Lady W—, which Miss Biggs would come creaking into the kitchen to collect when the panic was at its height. This morning was worse than usual. I generally tried to give the nursery something that I was going to cook for the dining-room so that I could do it all together, but today Mrs Lewis had ordered kidneys and mushrooms, which the nurses didn't fancy for the children, and scrambled eggs which couldn't be cooked before they were wanted. I decided to give them sausages and bacon, so I hoisted Polly from the floor to cut off bacon rinds and discovered that the big frying-pan that I wanted to fry the sausages in had not been washed, and bore traces of yesterday's smelts. I didn't dare tick her off in case it should send her queer, and I had no time to clean it myself, so I threw the sausages into the fishy fat and hoped for the best.

Nellie came in with one of her trays and said cheerfully: 'What a stink,' but I had no time to talk to anyone as I was trying to core kidneys, grill toast, heat porridge, make coffee, and watch the sausages and bacon all at the same time, as well as keep an eye on Polly, who was now peeling mushrooms with a dangerously sharp knife.

The least pleasant of the children, a smug little beast called Leonora, came prancing in at this point with her round face shining between tight sticking-out pigtails.

'Good morning, cook,' she remarked patronizingly. 'Nanny says she would like you to do some fried tomatoes for breakfast.'

'Oh, tell Nanny to go to the devil,' I said, and immediately regretted it, for the brat gave vent to a delighted 'Ooh!' and rushed off to repeat the naughty word. An infuriated nurse soon came bustling in, crackling with starch and indignation, saying: 'I don't wish to make trouble, cook, and if Leonora was not such a truthful child I could only hope that she had invented what she told me you said to her. I really must ask you to be more careful – such rudeness – a shocking example for children.' I hastily changed the subject. Banging a loaf of bread about and flourishing the bread-knife to put her off her stroke I said:

'I can't do you tomatoes, Nurse, because I haven't got any. William hasn't brought them in yet.'

'Oh, well, that's a pity I'm sure. What are you giving us? Sausages? I'm not very keen on sausages for growing children, you know.'

She was a college-trained nurse and full of theories

about food values, so I got rid of her by telling her that sausages were well known to contain all four vitamins, A, B, C, and D, to which she replied, 'Tchah!' and left the room in a fury.

That uniformed body of females, 'the Nurses', were always having a feud with someone. There were actually only three of them at Chilford House, but they made up for that by being an infernal nuisance. When they were not up against their employers about some detail of child upbringing they were making our life hell by sending back food from the nursery and demanding absurd delicacies at the most inconvenient times, not to mention flying in a horrified body to Mrs Lewis at the sight of a tiny speck of dust on the nursery floor. They were also incessantly at war with the children, who conducted a well-organized and admirable campaign for their discomfiture. They would hide in the tops of thick trees and call down mocking personalities as the nurses passed below, and cryptic notes hinting at shady pasts and unbelievable vices were left lying around all over the house.

Separately, these nurses may have been perfectly charming, but as a body antagonism seemed to be a *parti pris* with them.

Miss Biggs came into the kitchen as I was piling the nursery breakfast on to a huge tray for Rose to take in, snatching the dining-room coffee off the fire with one hand, just as it was boiling over.

'Good morning, Mrs Dixon,' she said, arranging Lady W—'s breakfast on her tray with maddening deliberation and accuracy of detail. 'Quite at sixes and sevens this morning, aren't we?' Mildred and Jessie, the parlour-maids, one a pretty local girl and the other a plain but efficient machine, came in for the dining-room breakfast before it was ready, and I pointed righteously to the huge clock which showed twenty minutes to nine.

'That clock's slow, always has been,' said Jessie.

'Hurry, Mrs Dixon, lovey, us'll have Mr Dawkes after we else,' said Mildred anxiously.

Even when they had departed, weighted down by trays heaped with mountains of food and gallons of coffee – why *do* people eat so much on holiday? – my work wasn't done. It was now time for the staff to have their break-fast, and, said my stomach, high time too. A mass of sausages had been sizzling on the range, but everybody always fancied a nice bit of fried bread, so that had to be done, and there was still Mrs Lewis's tray to be sent up. I used to keep something back from the dining-room for her, she couldn't very well say that it wasn't good enough, though she was very particular and would often refuse to eat what we were having in the kitchen. At last everything was done, down to the enormous brown pot of tea, and I slid thankfully into my worn plush chair at the servants' hall table. I used to keep some coffee back for myself, for in my opinion no day is a day that doesn't start with at least two cups of it. The other servants regarded me askance over this, they felt the same way about their cup o' tea, and 'Coffee?' they said, 'never touch it. Poison to the kidneys.' But oh! the joy of those first few mouthfuls, bringing comfort to the aching void created by rising early and working feverishly on an empty stomach.

Today was Nellie's and Rose's half-day, and they were discussing what they should do. For my part, when I got time off I used to go and sleep in a hedge somewhere, rejoicing to breathe a little pure air away from the greasy vapours of the kitchen or my smelly bedroom furniture. These two, however, with the energy of town-breds, wanted a whirl of gaiety which was not to be found in sleepy little Birching.

They generally used to rush off after lunch to catch the Birching bus which stopped at the end of the avenue, and would spend the afternoon strolling round the shops arm in arm and the evening at the small and smelly local cinema. If they couldn't get their work finished in time to catch the bus they would bicycle madly into the village to gaze into the window of the one general store which sold hardly anything except sweets and matches. Anything to get away from the boredom of rural scenery.

'Mouldy hole this is,' grumbled Nellie, biting into a huge door-step of bread and butter. 'Might as well not have a 'alf-day at all. Give me Torquay, that's more my style. Why, when I was at Torquay –'

We had all heard enough about Torquay, where Nellie had had her last place, to last us a lifetime – it was one of her pet subjects. Rose cut her short by saying:

'What say we get the bus, Nell? I want to match up some ribbon, and there's a Clark Gable at the Roxy.'

'It always means coming out before the end to catch the bus back, though. Last time we had to leave before the part where they discover it was all a misunderstanding. I *was* fed up. Tell you what, I'm fed up with this hole. Don't think I'll stay much longer. I'm going to tell that old cow straight out – it's not good enough I'm going to say.'

She leaned back, stretching her arms above her head and smiling complacently with the air of one who has made an impressive and startling announcement. Nobody took any notice, however; we all went on chewing as we'd heard all this before, too.

Nellie really didn't mean it herself, but she liked to hear herself talk, and she got up soon and went off yawning, to make beds.

Mildred helped to clear the table. Washing up the kitchen crockery was yet another of poor Polly's tasks, but when I went to look for her to clamp her to the sink she was nowhere to be found. I hunted everywhere for her, even in the coal cellar, where she always hid if there was a storm getting up or electricity in the air. I eventually discovered her sitting in a sort of coma on a big stone by the side of the back drive that led to the garage and stables.

'Polly! What on earth –?'

'Sh – go away.' She waved me aside without looking at me, and her fixed gaze became even more rapt as the big black Daimler turned out of the stable yard and swished majestically past us with her hero at the wheel.

I booted Polly back to the pantry where I left her, scraping egg off plates in an ecstatic trance. I had only time to make my bed in a slapdash way and change the water of my flowers before rushing back to the kitchen in time to be there when Mrs Lewis paid her state visit. It was a field day today for Miss Biggs, and I kept meeting her round corners or on the stairs and it gave her an opportunity to say: 'More haste less speed,' or 'All behind like the cow's tail,' each time I flashed by her.

When I got downstairs there was a strange male in a very dirty pair of grey flannels wandering about the kitchen. I thought at first that it was one of the tradesmen, but then I saw no bicycle clips and realized that it was one of the house party.

'I say,' he said, putting a handful of toast crusts into his face, 'could you possibly give me a bit of butter? I've practically burned my hand off on the exhaust pipe of my car.'

'Let's have a look,' I said, and he displayed quite a nasty place on the back of his hand. If he wanted butter on it well and good, it was not my place to suggest that he applied to Mrs Lewis who was in charge of a fully equipped medicine chest. She came in as I was holding his hand in mine and dabbing it with the best Unsalted, and was deeply affronted at one of her prerogatives being usurped.

'Hullo, Lulu,' said my patient, showing dizzy lack of respect, 'just being treated for burns.'

'You come straight up to my room, Mr Teddy, and have some carron oil on it. Butter indeed! Cook should know better than to risk infection like that. Quite absurd.'

'Oh, but Lulu –' He was dragged off, protesting, and dripping greasily over Polly's clean floor. I realized that he must be the eldest grandson. I ought to have known from his broken nose. It had been the subject of much speculation in the servants' hall. Dawkes had it on good authority that he had come by it in a brawl in an East End brothel. Jim Driver knew for certain that a car smash had caused it, but Nellie was of the opinion that Mrs Lewis had caught him a clout with the largest and heaviest crucifix one day when he tried to make love to her.

She soon came stalking back to the kitchen and vented her annoyance with me by ordering all the most troublesome dishes she could think of, such as *puréed* vegetables and *consommé*. She produced her trump card by saying that I was to make *crème brûlée* for dinner.

'I presume you know how to make it, Mrs Dixon?'

'Certainly I do, Mrs Lewis.' I wasn't going to let on that I had not even the slightest idea what *crème brûlée* was, and when she had gone I flew to my cookery books and hunted for the simplest description of how to make it. It apparently had to be left for four hours after being made, then coated with caramel and left for another four hours at least before being served. This meant that I would have to start it at once, so I had to abandon my idea of making the weekly batch of plum cakes. My first attempt was a curdled failure, and looked more like scrambled eggs than *crème brûlée*, so I put it in the dog's dinner plate and started again. Luckily there was always a huge jug of cream in the larder, sent down each day from the farm, and eggs abounded, so it didn't matter that yet another unsuccessful attempt found its way into the dog bowl before I got it right. It was now time to start doing things for lunch, and I wanted Polly to come and help me prepare vegetables, but she had disappeared again. I ran her to earth in one of the larders, busily engaged in washing the whole place down and scrubbing the shelves.

'Polly,' I said sternly, 'this is a fine time to be doing this sort of thing when I want you in the kitchen.'

'Mrs Lewis said I was to,' she said, biting her nails and looking at me with scared lunatic eyes.

I was furious with the housekeeper, but I had to control my wrath before Polly, who was on the verge of a breakdown, so I said:

'Well, never mind, you can leave it now. I'll make it all right with her. Come along now, Poll dear, and scrape a nice carrot for me. *That's* right.' I jollied her up, and had just got her going quite happily in the kitchen when we both had to knock off work as the rest of the staff came flocking in to the servants' hall to have their 'elevenses'.

It always seemed to me that breakfast was hardly over before everyone wanted to pack more tea and bread and butter inside themselves. It would not have been etiquette for me to absent myself from the gathering, however much I wanted to get on with my cooking, so I had to sit there, fretting at the waste of time. Not that I don't generally welcome any opportunity to stop work, but under the circumstances it only meant more panic afterwards trying to get things done in time.

Nellie and Rose were still talking about their plans for the afternoon and were having a rather tedious discussion as to whether Rose should wear her pink silk blouse with or without the coral beads.

Dawkes had apparently been having a very interesting morning going through the stumps of his employer's cheque books for the past year.

'That old devil's up to something,' he said. 'Two

hundred pounds to the Central Fur Stores. Lady W—never saw a hair of *that* partickler bit of rabbit, I'll bet.'

'Be your age, Mr Dawkes,' said Nellie, shattering his dream of scandal. 'Everybody knows that was a present he give Miss Dorothy on her twenty-first, so don't excite yerself.'

'Ah, Miss Clever, then what about "Mrs Eva Grant twenty pounds", and, farther on, "Mrs Eva Grant fifty pounds"? He never had a granddaughter by *that* name. Smells fishy to me. You mark my words, that old b— isn't above a bit of you know what, even at his age.'

Everybody drew in their breath and tut-tutted, except Polly, who was busily engaged in picking bits off the heel of her shoe. Miss Biggs always missed the implications of Dawkes' coarser remarks, so she wasn't as shocked as she should have been.

'Ah, well,' she said, rising with difficulty from a low chair, 'live and let live. It takes all sorts to make a world, you know, Mr Dawkes.' Licking her fingers she collected a few stray crumbs that she had missed round her plate, and hobbled off saying, 'Well, I must go and get my lady dressed.' Polly and I returned to our inferno of heat and bustle. The fire in the range was blazing away and I couldn't imagine ever having felt cold. By lunch-time I was limp and dripping and couldn't find the energy to be benign to a very small child who wandered in and walked round and round the kitchen saying, 'Choccy biccy, choccy biccy,' with maddening persistence.

Nellie and Rose fairly bolted their lunch, and didn't even stay to have a second jam tart, which was all to Miss Biggs' advantage. While I was shaking the tablecloth out of the back door I caught sight of them hareing across the short cut through the park to where the bus stopped. I couldn't see whether Rose was wearing the beads or not.

I generally had a bit of time to myself after lunch to 'put me feet up' or go out and get a bit of air, before I had to start making scones for tea.

Today, however, I had to make the cakes that should have been done in the morning, not to mention putting a caramel top on to the *crème brûlée*. This was rather fascinating, as all that had to be done was to sprinkle sugar heavily over the top, and put it under a very hot grill. It bubbled and heaved like the crater of a volcano and eventually turned a beautiful glassy brown.

'Sucks to you, Ma Lewis,' I thought, as I mixed plum cake in an enormous bowl. When I had filled the tins, I put them into the old-fashioned ovens to cook, and made up the fire well.

Polly had wandered out and I was wondering idly where she had gone, when my blood was frozen by a horrible yelling that grew louder as Polly flashed past the window and hurled herself into the kitchen, screaming:

'Fire! Fire! Oh, my Gawd! Oh, help! Fire, oh, help! Fire, fire, fire!'

'Where?' I said calmly, thinking that this was a figment of her disordered brain, but even as I spoke an ominous smell of burning drifted to my nose, and sure enough, a light rain of black ashes was falling outside the window. I rushed out and looking upwards saw that the kitchen chimney was indeed on fire and behaving like Vesuvius. Polly had followed me, still yelping, and before I could stop her, she had seized the rope that hung down outside the back door and was tolling away with desperate strength at the huge bell that was only rung for deaths and real emergencies.

The effect was dynamic. People appeared from everywhere in various conditions of excitement and horror. The old groom came galloping down the back drive on his bow legs just in time to catch Miss Biggs as she fainted stiffly away.

My friend with the burnt hand came running up with a gun that he had been cleaning, which added to the nurses' terror, and Sir Harold W— himself appeared in his braces and camel-hair slippers, having evidently been woken from his after-lunch nap. Nobody did anything; we all stood around and pointed and screamed. Someone hopefully brought out a fire extinguisher, but no one knew how to work it.

The children were enjoying themselves enormously,

but the excitement didn't last long. As it gradually dawned on us that the smoke and sparks were getting less and less, and that the fire was going out of its own accord, the tension relaxed, and the annoyance which relief often brings set in. Sir Harold suddenly realized that Polly was still pealing the bell, and he sprang at her with a roar of rage.

'Who's this crazy girl? She's the cause of all this ridiculous panic. Stop it, for God's sake, d'you hear me? Get rid of her, somebody, before I go raving mad. Dawkes! Don't stand there like a fool, man, *do* something. And then ring up the sweep and tell him to come over at once and see what's happened to the damned chimney.' He disappeared into the house, muttering oaths, and somebody plucked Polly off the rope and she stopped screaming, and bursting into hiccupping sobs, flung herself to the ground.

Nurses now began to slap and shake their various charges, and the bishop was heard to speak quite sharply to a fluttering lady in green, who insisted on clinging to his arm as they wandered away with the rest of the crowd; I went back to the kitchen lugging Polly with me, and the only figure left on the scene was Sir Harold's black spaniel who was quietly throwing up the curdled *crème brûlée* on to the drive.

The fire was of course the chief topic at tea-time in the servants' hall. Everybody wanted to give an opinion as to the cause of it. Mrs Lewis had apparently told Dawkes that she was certain it was something that I had put on the fire, though what it could have been, short of a can of petrol, I don't know. Miss Biggs was still a little prostrated and inclined to moan: 'We shall all be burned in our beds tonight, I know it.' She would not believe that the fire was really out until the sweep himself came down from his acrobatics on the roof to take a cup of tea with us, and assured her that there was no mortal peril. He had peered down the mouth of the great chimney, and had ascertained that the fire was out, but could not tell the cause or the extent of the damage without climbing up inside it from below.

'Yew'll have to let this yere fire out in the range tonight,' he said with his mouth full of sponge cake. 'I'll pop over early tomorrow and climb up her with me ladder.'

'Oh, what a nuisance,' I said, 'must you really?'

'Well, we must know the whoiy of it, mustn't us? Might happen again else.'

'Oh, don't say that,' pleaded Miss Biggs. 'I'm afraid you'll have to put up with the slight inconvenience, Mrs Dixon. One must suffer, you know, for the cause of many.'

I saw that there was no help for it. I should just have to get up at the crack of dawn to supervise the sweep and then light the fire when he had finished so that one or two people at least should get baths before breakfast.

We had to have a clean tablecloth after the sweep had gone, as he was not at all careful with his person, and had leant sooty elbows everywhere in a free and easy way.

I had to do all the cooking for dinner myself, as Polly was definitely written off for the rest of the day. She had wandered out into the shadows after tea, probably to hang round the garage for a sight of Jim Driver who had taken Lady W— out on an all-day visit. It was a lucky thing that she had missed the Great Fire, it might have upset her health even more than Miss Biggs.

Even though I started directly after tea, I only just got everything done in time. Mercifully, I didn't have to cook a hot dinner for the staff. Our main meal was lunch, and we always had cold meat or something in the evening, and chunks of soap-like cheese, washed down with the inevitable tea. The nurses had the same, with cocoa, sitting round the nursery fire with their knitting and their magazines on mothercraft. The dining-room dinner was generally quite an extensive affair, and tonight Mrs Lewis, just to complicate things a little, fancied a mush-room omelette for herself.

Nellie and Rose came bursting into the servants' hall as we were finishing our supper, and even the phlegmatic Rose was panting to hear the news.

'Tom told us on the bus that there'd been a fire – part of the roof fell in, he said.'

'Fancy us missing it, y'know,' said Nellie, regretfully.

'Just my luck to miss the only bit of excitement we've had here since the pipes burst.'

We disillusioned them about the size of the fire, but Nellie was still upset at having missed it, as they hadn't even enjoyed the cinema. The projection was dim, and the sound part had broken down half-way through, and even Clark Gable loses glamour when mouthing silently at you out of a thick fog.

I went upstairs early as I was worn out, and also the thought of the sweep's early visit was weighing heavily on my mind. Maddeningly enough, when I did get into my high iron bed, I couldn't sleep. The more I kept thinking that I must get to sleep, the more wakeful I became, and eventually I got sick of the clanging each time I tossed, and decided it was worth the effort of going down to the kitchen to get a hot drink. While the kettle was boiling, I thought it would be a good opportunity to explore the rest of the house, which I had never really seen.

It was after one o'clock, and all was still and dark on the farther side of the swing door as I crept through in my carpet slippers. I was quite enjoying myself roaming through the rooms pretending I was the family ghost when my phantom glide was turned into the most material somersault as I tripped over a gaitered leg that was protruding unexpectedly from the depths of an easy chair.

'God bless my soul,' said the astonished bishop, waking with a start from deep slumber. 'What? Where – ?'

'Oh, I *beg* your pardon, sir, I mean your worship, your reverence, that is,' I stuttered, picking myself up and backing out of the Presence. I could hear him following me, still mumbling and exclaiming, as he tried to brush pipe ash off his apron. I fled through the swing door to the refuge of my kitchen, drank my drink, and rushed upstairs and into bed as if pursued by a bogey man instead of a bishop.

Chapter Ten

After Easter the house party began to break up, and by the end of the holidays everybody except a few insignificant female relations and one or two of the younger children had gone. There were always guests at the week-end, but most of the time life was delightfully slack after the turmoil of work to which I had been accustomed. We grew fat and lazy in the kitchen, though Mrs Lewis still chivvied us around to keep us up to the mark. The pretty parlourmaid Mildred went home and the pantry maid ceased to appear every day, which meant that Polly didn't have any less to do, as she had no one to help her with all the kitchen washing up. I let her off helping me with the cooking, as she really wasn't much use anyway, and either hard work or unrequited love was making her look pasty and peaky. Jim Driver had got a girl in the village and he used to rush out like a dog every evening after supper and not return till quite late. He often went courting in one of his master's cars, and if I was still awake I would hear him from my room returning to the garage. He was lucky not to be discovered. Sir Harold's window was in the front of the house, and so was Mrs Lewis's, but somehow he always got away with it.

One evening, much to my surprise, Jim came into the kitchen while I was cooking the dinner and said shyly: 'Would you care to come for a wee drive this evening, Missis?'

I was too astonished to say 'No,' though I was rather scared at the thought of the risk of being seen in the borrowed car, and also I couldn't make out what had become of Bessie, his girl. 'You won't say anything to the others now?' he asked, jerking his head in the direction of the servants' hall.

'No, of course not,' I said, rather thrilled at the prospect of this clandestine outing. He really was quite good-looking, and as he went out I noticed that the boils on the back of his neck were almost completely cured.

After supper I made an excuse for going up early, saying I had to write letters. I changed my apron for something a little more glamorous, and crept out of the back door when no one was looking. Jim was waiting in the road just above the garage, and I got into the front seat of the Daimler beside him. I felt most opulent as we hummed along the lanes for a while in silence. Jim seemed nervous, and didn't talk much, and I didn't want to say anything until I had discovered why I had been invited. Eventually he decided that we had gone far enough, for he suddenly braked and brought the car to a standstill on the grass verge of the road.

He leant towards me, and I was just going to slap his face in the best manner when I saw it was a cigarette he was offering me, and not a passionate embrace. It was rather an anticlimax when I realized that I was not to be assaulted after all. When the cigarettes were lit, Jim leaned back in his corner and said:

'I brought you here for a wee talk. Would you mind very much giving me some advice?'

'All right by me,' I said, 'but why pick on me?'

'Well, Missis, if I was to take one of the other girls driving now, I'd be after kissing them instead of talking.'

I didn't quite know whether to take this as a compliment or a horrible slight, so I passed it over, and said:

'What d'you want my advice about? Is it Bessie?'

'It is.'

He poured out the whole story, and I must say I thought Bessie seemed rather a low character.

It appeared that although they had an understanding and were technically 'keeping company', she had ceased to dedicate all her evenings to Jim, and he was a seething mass of jealousy. Calling for her one day, he had met her just leaving the house arm-in-arm with a red-haired runt from the International Stores. Jim had made a scene, but Bessie had given him to understand that he had no proprietary rights, and had gone flouncing off with Ginger smirking at her side.

'I don't know what to do with the girl,' said Jim sadly. 'I love her, and I thought she loved me, but it's a queer way she's carrying on.'

It was a familiar story, so it didn't take me long to think of what to say.

'I think she's just going on like this for the fun of making you jealous – just to add a bit of spice to life, see? So I tell you what to do, Jim. You pay her back in her own coin. You get *her* jealous of *you*. Instead of going up there after her, you take somebody else out. She'll soon come screaming back to you if she thinks someone else is going to nab you.'

The more he thought about the idea the more he liked it. His wrath at the moment was greater than his love. 'I'll show her,' he said, 'I'll do her down. But ye'll have to help me. Will you come out with me, as a favour, somewhere where she'll see us?'

'Oh, Jim, I'd much rather not.' I didn't see why I should be involved in this romance. 'Take one of the girls out, can't you?'

'No, no, it must be you. It was your idea, anyway. How would I be explaining to them that I wasn't after walking out with them? I don't have to tell you that I wouldn't be asking you out if it wasn't for this.'

Another dubious remark, but nevertheless I realized I

would have to help him, as his mind seemed to be made up. We drove back to Chilford House debating when and where to spring the shock on Bessie. Jim had a marvellous idea. There was to be a dance at the Chilford Village Hall in a few days' time, to which Bessie was sure to be going, and it coincided with my evening out. He would be able to get off, as Sir Harold and Lady W— never went out in the evening.

We put the car in the garage as quietly as possible. The groom lived in a cottage out of earshot, and if the red-haired stable boy who slept above the garage with Jim heard anything, he would never say a word, as he was a trusted ally. I sneaked down the drive and got into the house by a secret way I had discovered through the coal cellar, and arrived black but undiscovered in my bedroom, beginning already to regret what I had let myself in for.

Jim and I had decided that we must keep the whole thing very dark, as there would be a lot of talk if it were discovered that we were going to the dance together. Our names would be coupled in the servants' hall. The atmosphere became rather tense, therefore, when at lunch the next day Miss Biggs suddenly piped up: 'I see there's to be a dance at Chilford on Thursday. Is nobody going to trip the light fantastic?'

'You bet I am,' said Nellie. 'I'm going with me beau, and what's more I'm going to wear all me jools.' Jim and

I looked at each other. It would wreck everything if Nellie was to crash in on our delicate plot. I couldn't make out whether she was joking or not.

'Are you really going, Nell?' I said, trying to sound casual.

'Course I'm not, dearie; where would I get a boy from in this dead-and-alive hole? Unless Mr Dawkes would like to take me – ?'

'Not in my line, I'm afraid,' said Dawkes, grinning. 'Kid's game, dancing, I always say.'

'And we all know Mr Driver has a date with an angel,' continued Nellie, 'so here I am on the shelf. When I think of the boys who used to take me out at Torquay – the Promised Land that was all right.'

'I can't think why you ever left your precious Torquay,' said Jessie dourly.

'Well, ducks, that's a subject over which we draw a veil,' said Nellie. 'It not being entirely to the credit of Yours Truly.'

I was glad to discover someone else besides me who had got the sack; I wasn't going to admit mine in public, but I made up my mind to have a discreet get-together with Nellie about it some time. One morning a few days later, I was lying in bed thinking about the fateful dance, when an awful thought suddenly struck me: 'My dear, I haven't a rag to wear!' Evening dress is not part of a cook's trousseau. All I had with me besides my aprons were one or two decayed-looking skirts and jerseys. I would not be busy that afternoon, so I made up my mind to go into Birching and 'look at the shops'.

When the others saw me hurrying lunch in order to catch the bus, there was a good deal of caustic comment.

'You goin' to town, Mae West?' said Nellie. 'Don't tell me you've found a young man, you lucky girl!' I couldn't help blushing guiltily, and they were all delighted. 'I do believe it's that handsome policeman at the cross-roads,' said Miss Biggs naughtily.

'How did you guess?' I said, getting up to go.

'If you can't be good, be careful!' screamed Nellie after me, as I ran up the back stairs.

I only just caught the bus and flung myself panting into a seat beside a fat farmer. I had recovered my breath by the time we got to Birching, but he was still puffing from the mere effort of being stout. Stepping down into the market square, I looked about me for a fashion salon.

There was a draper's shop on one corner, whose windows besides displaying balls of wool and innumerable lace collars, contained one or two rather depressed-looking dresses. One of them, a tasteful creation in pink sateen, had a label pinned across it saying 'à la mode', so I thought I would risk it. I opened the door and nearly knocked over a small man in pince-nez, who was waiting on the other side of it to direct customers.

'Which department, Madam?' he inquired, indicating with a wave of his hand a choice of three or four counters. 'I want to try that pink dress in the window,' I said.

'Ladies' Modes? Certainly, madam. Miss Smith, take madam to the Ladies' Modes.' A fuzzy-haired young woman with a heavy cold ushered me through a curtain into a little room at the back of the shop, containing two mirrors and an ash-tray. She brought me the dress and stood snivelling while I struggled into it. It might have been worse, even though it did make one think of 1920, when waists were somewhere round the hips. It would have to do for Chilford, though I doubted whether Bessie could possibly be jealous of Jim going out with a pink sateen dress that ended in a girlish frill about six inches from the ground.

'I'll take it,' I said, in spite of having just caught sight of my back view.

'It looks *lovely*,' said the sniffing one, sadly – 'ever so stylish.'

I smuggled it home and up to my room, and stored it carefully in the tin suitcase. I had decided that I couldn't possibly change at Chilford House without being discovered, so when the great day arrived, I borrowed Nellie's bicycle, giving them to understand that I had a heavy date with the policeman, and rode off after tea with my ball gown in a shopping bag on the handlebars. The 'Green Man' at Chilford provided me with a small dim room, in which I changed and did my face and hair as best I could. I felt far more terrified than a debutante at a state ball as I descended to the Private Bar where I was to meet Jim.

'How do I look?' I asked him, as I sipped my port and lemon.

'You look grand,' he said, chivalrously but doubtfully. He himself was looking smart and shiny in a blue serge suit, and I felt quite proud as we entered the village hall, gay with twists of coloured paper and bells left over from Christmas. 'The Four Happy Harmonists', in co-respondent shoes, were swinging it to the 'Lily of Laguna', so I took off my coat and Jim and I ventured a genteel foxtrot.

After about five minutes he suddenly pinched me, and I came to with a start from the trance that the combination of music and the smell of his hair oil was producing.

'She's here!' he breathed into my ear, and directed my gaze to the doorway. A buxom black-eyed girl was entering gaily on the arm of a small creature with red hair and a fatuous smile of pride.

'Hold me closer, Jim,' I whispered back, 'don't forget you've got to make her jealous.'

He clutched me fervently to his bosom, breathing heavily and falling over my feet in his emotion. I threw back my head with a fascinating smile of careless rapture, and had the satisfaction of seeing Bessie's jaw drop and her eyes blaze as we glided across her view. She tossed her head and danced off with Ginger, steering him deftly, as he was too small to see over her shoulder.

In the interval, I made Jim get me some fizzy lemonade, and sit by me in an attentive way, though his eyes kept swivelling round to where Bessie was chatting brightly and glancing at him covertly when she thought he wasn't looking.

My plan worked even quicker than I expected. One more passionate polka with Jim, and Bessie could contain herself no longer. At the end of the dance I skipped out of the door, and when I returned, five minutes later, the deed had been done. The pair of them were waltzing together, and if their feet were not always doing the same steps, their dreamy eyes were in perfect communion. Ginger had disappeared, presumably to drown his sorrows in the Green Man. Jim didn't even see me as he floated past ecstatically, so, having done my good deed, and feeling rather *de trop*, I decided to go home.

It was starting to rain when I got outside, and I was hanged if I was going to bicycle a mile and a half in 'my Ladies' Modes'. I felt I was entitled to some reward for my evening's work, so I hopped round to the public-house yard where Jim had left the Daimler, and drove myself home in style.

After all he had Love, so I didn't see why I shouldn't have Luxury.

*

Life was almost too gay. Not long after the village dance, I began to hear talk of what was apparently an annual event at Chilford House – a Servants' Ball at Whitsun. The house was to be full again over the long week-end, and family, guests, and staff would mingle with a great deal of embarrassment on all sides, and dance in the big hall to the strains of the Happy Harmonists.

There was a lot of discussion and excitement in the kitchen regions. Mildred and the pantry-maid had returned in preparation for the house party, and a stout old charlady came every day and swelled our gathering at the lunch table.

Nellie was going to wear red taffeta at the dance, and was hoping to pinch the broken-nosed Teddy from Mildred, who had had conspicuous success with him the year before.

'Did he reely kiss you behind the coats in the lobby, Mil?' she said one day when we were, as usual, discussing the topic of the hour.

'Mm,' said Mildred, blushing furiously.

'How lovely. Wait till he sees me in me red. He'll go for me in a big way, see if he don't.'

'Pride comes before a fall,' said Miss Biggs. 'Don't talk so shocking, Nellie.'

'Who else is going to be there, anyway?' Nellie asked Dawkes. 'Any guests coming except pot-bellied old geezers with flat feet?'

'One or two,' said Dawkes, who had evidently been through his employers' entire correspondence on the subject. 'Mr and Mrs Wilson-George – that dame with the fancy sparklers; the Gregorys – dirty spongers – mean as hell, no tip from them. A bloke from London – friend of Mr Teddy's, I think –'

'New Blood, eh? What's his name?'

'Let's see. Robin something or other – Brook – no Burke, Robin Burke.'

All eyes were turned on me as I choked on a fish-bone and was very nearly sick on the table. I fled from the room, thankful for an excuse to hide my horror. This was terrible! What a ghastly situation, to be cook in the house where one of the guests was to be an old flame of two years ago, and to come face to face with him at the Servants' Ball wearing pink sateen, and black strap shoes. I could not possibly go to the dance. Apart from the embarrassment of meeting him, it would lead to all sorts of complications and explanations below stairs. On the morning of the dance, I appeared at breakfast with my right foot heavily bandaged and encased in a carpet slipper. There were cries of sympathetic inquiry from all sides.

'Spilt some boiling water on it,' I explained. 'Just my rotten luck. No dancing for me.'

'Well, you are a wounded warrior!' cried Miss Biggs. 'Never mind, you shall sit with me, and we'll watch the young folk enjoying themselves.'

I was disappointed to hear that she was not going to dance. I had had visions of her doing the Rumba, clicking out the rhythm on the bones of her stays. I said: 'Not me – I'm not going to come to the rotten show if I can't dance. I shall go to bed and pray for you all.'

I really was disappointed at not being able to go; I had been looking forward to my spot of gaiety. It was just like Robin to turn up at a time like this. He had always been possessed of a charming lack of tact.

I hopped and limped about the kitchen all day, and my other leg became quite crippled under the strain. I had been very busy for the past few days making refreshments, and there was still a lot to do on the day of the dance. By five o'clock I was thankful to sink into a chair and revive myself with tea. The others looked pretty dead too, they had been hard at it all day under the eye of Mrs Lewis, and Nellie voiced the feelings of everybody when she said:

'I'm not sure that this hop isn't more trouble than it's worth. I feel more like goin' to bed and sleeping for a week than prancing round the ballroom on me poor dogs.'

'Hear, hear,' said Rose. 'I quite envy Mrs D. her scald.' Dawkes, who had gone to answer the telephone, came back at this moment, and said gleefully to Nellie:

'Got a disappointment for you, my girl. Mr Burke's just phoned to say his car's broke down and he won't be here till morning.' 'Oh, it's too much,' said Nellie, pouting. 'Just when I was all set for Romance. I shall have to make a go for that sissy curate. It's me last chance.'

I was delighted. All I had to do now was to effect a quick and plausible cure on my foot and I would be able to go after all.

I got up and went to the door, reducing my limp considerably. 'My foot's ever so much better this evening,' I said brightly. 'I think I'll just pop up and put some more ointment on it. I might be able to come after all. You never know, I might cut you out with the curate yet, Nell.'

They seemed to take this all right, so as the evening drew on I gradually got less and less lame. Each time somebody poked their head into the kitchen to say: 'How's the foot?' I gave more and more cheering bulletins, till at last I was able to announce that I was coming after all, 'if my foot doesn't turn on me.'

There was no proper dinner to cook for the dining-room; they had a cold buffet, in order to give us a chance to get cleared up and changed by nine o'clock, when the guests were due to arrive. Both servants and employers had been asked from houses in the neighbourhood; class consciousness would be thrown to the winds, and a good time enjoyed by all. After dinner Dawkes and the girls had to put out the refreshments and drinks on long tables in the dining-room, and Polly and I converted the servants' hall into a ladies cloak-room for the visiting maids.

We all went up to change and there was much giggling and shrieking and running in and out of each other's rooms to lend a hand with pins and give gasping admiration. My pink concoction had quite a success. 'Sweetly pretty' was the verdict. I had to keep away from Nellie, as it clashed horribly with her red. She had gone very festive about the hair. She had curled it tightly with the tongs and then brushed it out into a stiff frizz, into which artificial poppies were stuck at random. I thought I would like to give myself a new coiffure, so I rashly chopped some off the front with nail scissors, and, borrowing Nellie's tongs, gave myself a fringe like a pantomime juvenile. We all collected in the kitchen, pushing and nudging, and much too shy to take the plunge through the green baize door.

Polly was wearing a trailing black dress that was too big for her and hung on her skinny frame as if it would fall off at any moment. I think it must have once belonged to Lady W— for it was certainly not a dress for anyone under seventy, but Polly had added glamour to it by spilling a bottle of vile-smelling Ashes of Roses over herself. She was scared stiff and clutched me in a panic when Dawkes swished into the room, resplendent and Mephistophelian in white tie and tails, and said: 'Get a move on, the beauty chorus; the Bish wants to open the ball with Miss Biggs.'

He led us giggling and jostling into the hall, where the Happy Harmonists were in full swing, and a terrifying number of rather blasé-looking people in evening dress were standing about in a tired way. We clustered by the stairs like sheep, wondering what to do with our hands, and were joined by the nurses, self-conscious but fearfully genteel in lace or art crêpe, with a great many scarves and handkerchiefs trailing about. Etiquette demanded that Sir Harold should open the ball with Mrs Lewis, while Dawkes seized the eldest daughter of the house, a stout matron in black velvet, and trundled her deferentially round the room. Once these two couples were started, anyone else could dance. A few staff guests had arrived and were coming through from the back regions, pushing us forward into the room. Teddy made for Mildred, and though Nellie hypnotized the curate with her eye, he was much too nervous to attempt anything just yet, so she accepted a sun-dried colonel from Chittagong, and bounced off with him. Would it be me for the bishop? I wondered, but then a young man with protruding teeth and no chin bore down on me and said, 'Will you tread a measure?'

'I don't mind if I do,' I said, wondering whether I had to call him 'Sir' or not. He was not a very good dancer and we fell over each other's feet rather a lot. Afterwards he got me some lemonade and obviously felt that he had done his duty by me. He stood fingering his tie for a little, but could not bring out any conversation from behind those rabbit teeth, so hastily disappeared into the crowd leaving me still wearing my fixed social smile.

A footman from Birching Manor approached and whirled me efficiently into a waltz. He danced perfectly, and I thought he was probably an ex-night-club gigolo. We got on rather well together, and he called me 'Toots'. We had another dance, and then he suddenly spied a rather lovely expensive-looking woman standing by herself; so he left me hurriedly to grab her while he had the chance. After this I danced with a small boy of sixteen whose mother made him ask me, and then one or two old buffers who thought they were being very gay and devilish. A rather forced gaiety had been established, and the dance might be said to be going with a swing. Nellie had lost most of the poppies from her hair, and Polly's stockings were round her ankles. I was really quite enjoying myself, when suddenly everything turned upside down and my heart missed about twenty beats. There in the doorway, more attractive than ever, stood an all too familiar figure. He had evidently got his car mended earlier, and had just arrived, for he was not wearing evening dress.

My ancient dancing partner was asking me a question which I couldn't answer, as I was too busy feeling sick and wondering how to escape. Would Robin recognize me? I saw his eye travel over the assembly, looking for his host. I buried my face in my old man's shirt front, but I saw out of one eye that Robin was staring at me with an expression of dawning amazement.

'Excuse me,' I gasped, and releasing myself from my partner's clutch, I bolted through the crowd like a rabbit, burrowing for the safety of the baize door. I didn't care what anyone thought, my one idea was to get away. There was someone on the back stairs, and I couldn't go up there, so I shot into the kitchen and flattened myself behind the door. It was not long before I heard the clatter of running feet on the stone passage, and Robin rushed into the kitchen, and, not seeing me, went across the room and through the door that led into the pantry. He would see me if he came back the same way, so I escaped and rushed along the passage to the servants' hall. All the rooms in the kitchen quarters led into each other, they made three sides of a rectangle, with the long passage as the fourth side, and as I went in at one end of the room, Robin appeared from the pantry at the other end. 'Hi!' he shouted, as I retreated hastily, 'Hi, stop!'

I heard a crashing of chairs, as he bounded after me, and I came to a skidding stop at the end of the passage, and popped into a larder before he could see where I'd gone. I heard his feet in hot pursuit, and he opened a few doors, but I risked it and stayed where I was. Eventually he panted into my larder and I just had time to escape through the other door into the kitchen before he could grab me.

'Stop!' he shouted again, as I raced for the pantry. 'Monty! Stop! What the hell d'you think you're playing at?' Round we went again, through pantry and servants' hall, down the passage, into the kitchen, and round again, and I was getting exhausted.

Desperately I pounded down the passage on the last lap, turned a corner beyond the kitchen, and went to ground in the coal cellar.

Robin fell through the door and down the steps after me, and the rest was a confused delirium of tweed coat, gasps, and coal dust.

Chapter Eleven

The rest of the weekend was rather a strain on my nerves, as I had to cope with Robin, who didn't seem to take kitchen etiquette half seriously enough. I had to speak to him severely about penetrating through the green baize door, and finally beg and implore him to consider my reputation.

He came prancing in one day, when Polly was with me in the kitchen, and said: 'Good morning, Cook. I wish to lodge a complaint about the food; there was a slug in my spinach at lunch, and the horse we had for dinner last night was high.'

Polly goggled and gasped, and I did a lot of shushing and pointing, and said out of the side of my mouth: 'Shut up! She's not as crazy as all that; she thinks it all most peculiar.'

'What do you do on your evenings out?' continued Robin, unabashed. I threatened him with a carving knife, dripping blood from the corpse of a rabbit, and at that moment Mrs Lewis walked in and stopped in her tracks, scandalized. She had been unreasonably annoyed about the Teddy episode, but this made the chains and crosses on her bosom rise and sink with real fury. She had an almost feudal sense of propriety and class consciousness, and she apparently thought I was 'making free' with the Gentry, which to her was the ultimate offence. It would not have been proper for her to have ticked me off in front of one of the guests, and equally well she could not turn him out, so she held her ground, a repressed mass of rage, still heaving with a sort of 'Jingle Bells' rhythm. Robin just stood grinning sheepishly, and didn't help me out at all. It was left to me to do something to break up the petrified silence.

'The gentleman wants some lard for his fishing line,' I said wildly, inventing the first thing I could think of. It didn't sound any more plausible to Mrs Lewis than it did to me, however, and she turned to Robin with an iron-ical smile.

'Indeed? And how are the fish rising, Mr Burke? I didn't know Sir Harold had restocked the lake, since all the fish died last year when the drains leaked in.'

My unfortunate excuse had exhausted my inventive powers, so I winked at Robin with the side of my face farthest away from Mrs Lewis, and he suddenly came up to the scratch most unexpectedly.

'Oh, well, you know, I wasn't thinking of doing any fishing here, unless I have a try for the gold-fish in the lily pond, ha, ha, what?' he said heartily, rubbing his hands.

'I'm going up to stay on the Tay tomorrow, you see, so I just wanted to get my rod ready.'

'One of the men could easily have done that for you, sir. If you'll tell me where it is I'll get Joseph to see to it at once.' She was suspiciously anxious to see the mythical rod, and kept turning her searching gaze from me to Robin in her effort to discover whether we were deceiving her.

'Oh, no, Mrs Lewis, please don't bother,' he said hastily, 'you see, it's a very special rod, my grandfather gave it me last year, and I don't really like anyone else to handle it, thanks awfully all the same – er – yes – er – well – thanks again –' He sidled to the door and bolted out, having done his bit, even if he did forget to take the lard. Mrs Lewis was still slightly dubious, but she left it at that and reverted to the other little bone that she had come down to the kitchen to pick with me. It was only a small matter of removing the fat from soup before sending it into the dining-room, but she elaborated it into quite a criminal offence, and left me crushed and apologetic.

The house party broke up on the evening of Whit-Monday, and I breathed a sigh of relief when I got rid of the embarrassment of Robin. He managed to drive away when Mrs Lewis wasn't about, so that she wouldn't notice the absence of the fishing rod, and I really thought that nobody suspected anything, except perhaps Polly, and she didn't count. A rude shock was in store for me, however.

One day at lunch Nellie started to talk about a book she had got out of the twopenny library. 'Ever so lovely, it is, makes me cry buckets.'

'What's it about?' asked Mrs Coombe, the charlady, who couldn't read or write her own name, but nevertheless took a deep interest in literature.

'It's all about a Dook hoo falls in love with one of his mother's maids. Her pride is her barrier, and she turns him down, but he wears her down with obstinate persistence, and they elope. Mind you, he does the right thing by her, it's that sort of book.'

'Isn't that beautiful?' said Mrs Coombe, gazing round the table with moist eyes. 'Wish I was educated like you, Nell. My Will's a rare one for books, though; he sometimes reads me the comical pieces in the papers – 'Itler and that. What do they call your tale?'

'*Flames of Desire*.'

Dawkes gave a scornful guffaw. 'Fancy you stuffing yourself with that rot. You'll get ideas above your station, my girl. No toff ever did right by a skivvy yet, in my experience. The other thing perhaps, and *not* a 'undred miles from this spot neither.'

'Why, whatever do you mean, Mr Dawkes?' said the charlady, and Nellie said, ''Ere, 'ere, 'ere, what you getting at, you nasty old man?'

'Oh, no offence, no offence,' he said, and they calmed down, thinking that this was just another of his usual incidental coarsenesses, but I suddenly realized with a shock of horror that he was having a dig at me. His narrowed eyes were fixed on me and said, as clearly as if he had spoken, 'I got something on you, my girl.'

He had evidently discovered the harmless truth of my little secret, and had characteristically inferred the worst. Why is it that one always blushes when one is innocent? Nobody else noticed my loss of composure, but Dawkes obviously thought it was an indication of guilt. The bell rang from the library, and he treated me to a slow and extremely sinister wink before rising and leaving the room. I felt quite sick at the thought of the ideas that were churning in the slime of his filthy mind. I decided that I would tackle him and vindicate my honour at the earliest possible opportunity.

He purposely avoided seeing me alone for a day or two, until he considered that he had got me sufficiently worked up by suggestive glances and odd words thrown here and there, unnoticed by the others, but most unnerving for me.

One afternoon, however, as I was going down through the shrubbery for a moody stroll in the park, he suddenly slid out from behind a laurel bush and fell into step beside me.

'Well?' I said, walking on without turning my head.

'Well – Monty –?' he replied insinuatingly. 'I've got a pretty tale stored up inside here,' tapping his head. 'Who am I goin' to tell it to, eh? Mrs Lewis, she might be amused, and why not Sir 'arold himself? He always appreciates my funny stories.'

'Why, you dirty, double-crossing rat!' I said, having spent my last half-day seeing a gangster film at the local cinema, 'there's not a bit of truth in your filthy insinuations, and you can't prove a thing.'

'Oho! So I suppose you and Mr Burke are total strangers, eh? Nothing between you at all?'

'More or less.'

'Well, I seen what I seen, and I'm damned if I'm going to keep it to meself. Unless –'

'Unless what?'

'You know what. You gotter make it worth my while, see?'

We had come to the gate into the park by now, and I opened it, trying to keep calm, and went through, leaving him to shut it and follow me over the long grass.

'I'm still not scared,' I said, when he had caught me up. 'I've got a perfectly clear conscience in spite of you trying to make me nervous. I'll tell you the whole truth, as I've really got nothing to hide. Mr Burke and I were friends not so very long ago, and he recognized me and wanted to talk to me. There's nothing in that. It's all perfectly normal.'

'Go on laughed Dawkes derisively. 'Tell that to someone else. Who's going to believe that Mr Burke had a platonic and social acquaintance with a cook? Them things don't happen outside of Nellie's books.'

'But don't you see –?' I began, but stopped, as it was hopeless to try and explain. I was all confused, and couldn't cope with the situation. One's education doesn't provide for dealing with things like blackmail. The safest way was to be thoroughly up-stage, so I said icily: 'I refuse to discuss the matter any further,' quickened my steps to get away from him, and, tripping over a mole-hill, sat down heavily on the wet grass.

'Well, dearie,' said Dawkes, when he had recovered from his transports of mirth. 'I'll give you a little time to think it over. We'll come to terms tomorrow. Meanwhile, I got me work to do. Ta-ta! Sweet dreams!' He strode away on his long legs, looking like a man-eating spider, and I remained where I was, getting damper and damper while I grappled with a desire to yell and scream with rage.

That night I slept on it, as the saying is, and, waking early, found the solution crystal-clear in my brain. I would pack up my tin suitcase and go. Once I had given notice, it would not really be worth Dawkes' while to broadcast his bit of dirt, and even if he did, I should not be there long enough for it to affect me. I had put aside quite a tidy little nest-egg out of my wages, as the pink creation had been almost my only expenditure, and I was not going to be blackmailed into parting with it. Although I had had a highly diverting and illuminating time at Chilford House, I felt I could do with a sight of my home again; there was so much to tell everyone, and I really was getting very sick of my clothes.

When Mrs Lewis came into the kitchen that morning, I took a deep breath and said: 'I'm afraid I must give notice. We have sickness at home; my sister's been taken with Pneumonia. Double, it is.'

'Well, that *is* aggravating,' she said. 'I don't like having to make changes all the time. Are you sure you must go?'

'Of course I must,' I said, as deeply affronted as if my sister really were lying at death's door and calling for me. 'People don't have Double Pneumonia every day, you know.'

'Oh, dear, it really is too trying. I suppose you'll stay until I can get someone to fill your place?'

'Oh, yes, of course, if you get someone quite soon,' I said. 'Why don't you try locally, in Exeter or somewhere? It would save a lot of time.' I marvelled at the way I was actually daring to dictate to her. Now that I was soon going to be out of her power, her domination didn't impress me at all, and when she said: 'That will do, I know my own business, thank you,' I merely laughed vulgarly as she went out of the room.

That know-all, Dawkes, knew almost as soon as I did

that I had given notice, and I was careful to keep out of his way until I could get some intimation from Mrs Lewis of when I would be able to go. His face was black with rage at lunch-time and he hardly spoke a word. Once or twice he opened his mouth as if he were going to denounce me publicly, but thought better of it, and evidently decided to wait and see whether he couldn't, after all, get something out of me.

Jim Driver was told to take Mrs Lewis into Exeter in the afternoon, so she had evidently taken my suggestion, and when she got back, I had the honour and distinction of being summoned to her room. It was rather a nuisance, as I was very involved at the moment with a Dressed Crab, about which Mrs Beeton and my French cookery book were contradicting each other. However, the opportunity of seeing the temple of prayer was not to be missed, so I sped upstairs, wiping my hands on my apron. I knocked at the door and went in, to find Mrs Lewis sitting at her desk, still wearing an unsociable black hat of shiny straw, perched high on her head. I had expected to find a mass of religious pictures, effigies, prie-dieus, and so forth, but, if Mrs Lewis prayed to any images, it must have been to the unflattering portraits of a host of fearsome relatives which covered the walls and furniture. The men were mostly whiskered, or walrus-moustached, with hair *en brosse*, and the women large, black, and forbidding. They were the sort of photographs that always give the impression that the people in them have departed this life, not so much from the age of the picture, but from the general air of the improbability of their being human; and if this lot weren't dead, they certainly ought to have been. I detached my gaze from Uncle Hugo on the mantelpiece, in the full-dress uniform of an undertaker's mute, as Mrs Lewis was addressing me.

'I am thankful to say that I have found someone in Exeter who will *more* than adequately fill your place. I have arranged for her to arrive tomorrow afternoon, and I should like you to show her the routine, such as you have followed, and where to lay her hands on everything, so please put the kitchen in order. Then you can go by the evening train. You have not had your wages yet for last week, so, as you are leaving without notice, the question of money does not arise.'

I didn't think she was being very kind to someone whose nearest and dearest was dying of Pneumonia, so I said, 'O.K.' and let her have another of my coarse laughs, which I knew grated on her gentility, and, with a smirk at Uncle Hugo, went out of the room banging the door behind me. I ran into Dawkes in the corridor, and still feeling vulgarly light-hearted, I buttonholed him. 'Well, old cock,' I said, 'I'm going tomorrow. Whatcher think of that? Puts an end to your "coming to terms", don't it?'

He stood there, biting his thumb savagely. 'I'll make

your name mud before you go, you little b—,' he muttered, 'and what's more, I'll see that it don't escape your folks neither. If you *have* a respectable family, that is, which I doubt.'

'Oh, they won't mind at all,' I said, 'a spot of poison pen means nothing to them. So if you – ' At this moment the door of Sir Harold's room suddenly opened, so I fled for the back stairs, leaving Dawkes to do his worst on the spot if he chose. As a matter of fact, I don't think he ever said a word to anyone – I certainly never heard anything about it. He probably never intended from the start to carry out his threat – he thought that he would be able to scare me into transferring my pitiful little earnings from my pocket to his. He was not really cut out for blackmail, for he was too small-souled ever to carry anything through.

A gratifying concern was shown in the servants' hall when I announced at supper that I was leaving the next day. All except Dawkes, who again sat cloaked in rage, showed a deep and slightly morbid interest in the Double Pneumonia story.

'Pneumonia?' said Miss Biggs, with sad relish, 'that's bad. They do say that even if it doesn't bring you to your grave, it leaves its mark on you for life. Has she had her crisis yet, poor soul?'

'Coming at any moment, I believe,' I said, earnestly.

'It's a pity she didn't have it right at the beginning,'

she went on, 'otherwise the disease takes its toll of your strength. My aunt took Pneumonia three years ago, and the crisis didn't come for quite a time, and afterwards she couldn't keep a thing down, and there are certain foods she can't hold to this day, if you'll pardon my mentioning it.'

'I'm sure we're ever so sorry for you, Mrs D.,' said Nellie. 'It's a real shame you've got to go, just when we was all getting on so well together. We shall miss you, shan't we, girls?'

The murmur of assent wasn't deafening, but it was enough, with Nellie's genuine sentiments, to make me feel rather mean to be getting their sympathy undeservedly.

I excused myself early, saying that I must go and pack, for I did not feel equal to staying for the usual gossip over the fire, to the accompaniment of a medley of clicks from Miss Biggs' knitting needles, teeth, and stay-bones. As I didn't know anything about Pneumonia, it was getting a bit difficult to discuss the symptoms of the case with that wealth of detail that seemed to be expected.

When I got upstairs, I discovered that three of my aprons were at the wash. I would ask Nellie to send them on to me, as I was not going to have the paragon from Exeter, whose name appeared to be Mrs Macbonn, swanking round the place in them. I set my alarm for an earlier hour than usual as I would have quite a lot to do tomorrow if I was to get the kitchen and larders into good enough order to save my self-respect when she arrived. The combination of Polly and me was not one calculated to make for cleanliness or tidiness. Apart from the fact that we were both messy by nature, I never seemed to have time to put anything away in its right place, and though any governess will tell you that it is just as quick to put a thing where it should go as where it should not, I have never found it so. When it means making treks down stone passages to put cheese in one larder and eggs in another, to satisfy the dictates of tradition, it becomes very unpractical.

When I woke for the last time in my little room, and inhaled its well-known smell with my first conscious breath, I felt quite a pang of regret at leaving these familiar surroundings. I felt it even more when I got up and went to the window to take a last look at the long stretch of green lawn and parkland, damp and fresh in the clean air of early morning. However, I had more important things to do than stand around in my nightdress admiring the beauties of nature. Polly was not yet about when I got downstairs, so I started in on the store cupboards in the kitchen, which were in a hopeless mess. None of the various tins, which held such things as spices and seasonings, seemed to have their lids on properly, and the paper on the shelves was encrusted with a sticky mixture of spillings from everywhere. I would have to put fresh paper down, so I took everything out, and all sorts of treasures turned up in odd corners. I discovered a lump of cheese walking about with its outside covered with a decorative green fluff; and a jar of pickles with grass growing on the top, and probably mushrooms too. All the sugars and things were in their wrong containers, and there was an old, unopened packet of Demerara hard as rock, which I had to attack with a rolling-pin. All this took time, and I only managed to get one cupboard superficially respectable, before it was time to start cooking the breakfast. Polly was on hands and knees as usual; she always cleaned floors in preference to anything else, as she seemed to prefer being on all fours – back to nature, I suppose.

Feeling a last-minute mellowness towards everyone, I hashed up a most appetizing kedgeree for the dining-room, accompanied by large, whole kidneys, whose juicy succulence was in no way impaired by the fact that I had dropped them off the grill on to the floor in my zeal. I even had a belated rush of tenderness for the nurses, and enlivened their boiled haddock with a few tomatoes. My *bonhomie* didn't extend as far as Mrs Lewis, however, as she had already made herself a nuisance by demanding an omelette, so I decided to let her wait for it until I had done all the breakfasts. Her bell began to ring before I had finished cooking our kippers, and continued to peal intermittently till Nellie went up to calm her down. She came back to the kitchen to report: '"Where's my break-fast?" she says. "It's ten minutes late!" I felt like telling her to pray for it – Manna, you know – but I daresay she can't pray on an empty stomach, so buck up, dearie, or I shall get what for, and you won't be the only one around here to get the push.'

'What do you mean?' I said, affronted. 'I didn't get the sack, I gave in me notice.'

'Only my fun, ducks, only my fun. Oh, for God's sake!' as the bell started again. 'She's at it again. Get a move on before we all go cuckoo.'

I obliged, and left the kippers, to throw an untidy-looking omelette together, and Polly clattered away with the tray. Mrs Lewis behaved exactly as if it was a day like any other when she came down to order the food. She never unbent to me at all in view of my imminent depar-ture; I supposed I should see her to say good-bye later on. I wondered whether I would have to say good-bye or anything to Lady W— before I left, but as I had never even said hullo when I arrived, it seemed a little unnec-essary.

I put Polly on to cleaning out the larders and making them look a bit more sanitary. I myself had to tidy away everything in my bedroom, as well as do a lot of cooking, so I couldn't do any more in the kitchen, and only hoped that Mrs Macbonn wouldn't be too critical.

She arrived soon after lunch, tall, gaunt, and grim,

with a hold-all grasped in each of her bony red hands and a man's felt hat skewered to her iron-grey bun by a steel hat-pin. She was desperately efficient. She marched up to her room straight away to gird herself for the fray, and came down looking like an armoured car in the starchiest and most aggressive apron ever seen. I gave her several rather sickly grins of an unnatural heartiness in an effort to jolly her up, but it was no good. She tramped behind me as I took her on a tour of the kitchens, commenting only in disapproving monosyllables. She hardly glanced at the cupboard that I had turned out that morning, but fixed a steely gaze on such things as the spoon drawer, and the other store cupboard, which I hadn't had time to do. Polly had evidently got sick of cleaning out larders, for she had abandoned the last one half-way through. She had put the food on to the floor in order to scrub the shelves and there it still sat: a ham, an apple pie, three cold sausages, and a piece of Gruyère, mutely imploring Mrs Macbonn not to be too hard on it.

When we got back to the kitchen we faced each other in the middle of the floor, and I smiled deprecatingly, but she just gave me one long withering look of pity, and then, turning away, was suddenly transformed into a whirling dynamo of frenzied activity. She fell on the cupboard like a madwoman, and started to clear out its contents with raking sweeps. 'Pardon,' she said, knocking into me as I got in her way. 'Granted,' I replied, and removed myself dispiritedly to the servants' hall, where I sat kicking the table legs and listening to her hurrying back and forth among the larders and pantries on her purgative mission.

I had meant to offer to help her cook the dinner, but now I saw that I should be more of a hindrance. She had taken complete possession of my kitchen, so she could jolly well stew in her own juice. When tea-time came, however, I thought I had better go in and tell her about heating up the scones that I had made. It was superfluous as she had already discovered them, and though they were, admittedly, a bit moth-eaten, I was distinctly outraged when I saw that she had gone so far as to throw them away and make a fresh batch of her own. When I went in she was just taking them out of the oven, with much deft flourishing of cloths and oven trays, and I was even more infuriated to see that she had made a perfect batch, risen up to a beautiful lightness, all neat and shapely, with glazed brown tops. Swallowing my jealous resentment, I forced myself to say brightly: 'What lovely scones, Mrs Macbonn! I'm afraid you're putting me to shame.'

'Ah, well,' she said tight-lipped, 'you'll learn some day, I expect.'

'I'm afraid you found the place rather untidy,' I pursued, mortifying myself still further for the good of my soul.

She became even more righteous: 'Well, of course, it's not at *all* what I've been accustomed to, but I'll soon get things straight, I daresay. I'm afraid I never *could* do with disorder round me, but we can't all be made the same way. Where's the kitchen-maid? Surely she should be here helping me?'

'I always let her go off in the afternoon, as there really isn't much to do. She's a bit – you know – ' I tapped my forehead, 'and she likes to wander about outside. She'll be back in time for her tea.'

'Well, we'll soon alter *that*,' said Mrs Macbonn grimly. 'There are one or two things that will have to be reorganized around here, I can see that.'

I wished her joy of reorganizing Polly, who would undoubtedly go over the top at the first word; but I also felt desperately sorry for the poor girl at the mercy of this horse-faced woman.

'Oh, *please*,' I begged, '*please* be nice to Polly. She means so well, and she can't help being a bit peculiar. You'll upset her dreadfully if you say anything to her, so *please* do be kind.'

'I hope I shall treat her with the fairness which I am accustomed to show to those around me,' she said, raising the iron-grey bars of her eyebrows; 'we should all get what we deserve in this life, no more, no less. Incompetence or slovenliness is abhorrent to me.' There was not much hope for poor Poll then, so I gave it up and went into the servants' hall where the others were sitting waiting for their tea.

'What's she like?' asked Rose, making a face in the direction of the kitchen.

'Oh, divine,' I said; 'you'll love her merry little ways.'

Mrs Macbonn came in at this moment, followed by Nellie bearing the teapot. 'Where do I sit, please?' she inquired, and was given my seat beside Dawkes, while I went and sat below the salt with Polly. The atmosphere was rather strained. For one thing, Dawkes was still broody as long as I was about, and the Macbonn was unpromising material for whoopee. Stiff as a girder, she sat dispensing tea, our polite conversational remarks rebounding off her like bullets off sheet-iron. Tomorrow was Sunday, and Miss Biggs was talking about the vicar's beautiful sermons.

'Perhaps you would like to come with me to church, Mrs Mactart?' she said kindly. 'Lady W— always sends us in the Morris with Joseph. May I ask what persuasion you are?'

'Thank you,' said Mrs Macbonn, turning not only her head but her whole body round to Miss Biggs, 'but I live my religion in my life. If I wish to say my prayers I can perfectly well do so in an open field.'

The staggering vision that this conjured up definitely quenched the feeble spark of conversation, and though one or two people tried to revive it by tentative throat clearings, it was no good. I looked at the clock and was thankful to see that it was time for me to go and get my things on if I was to catch my train. When I came down again Mrs Macbonn had retired to the kitchen, so I was able to say good-bye to the others in a less restrained atmosphere. Dawkes had gone to remove the drawing-room tea, so, when no one was looking, I placed in his chair the inverted drawing-pin that I had been saving up for this purpose. Prep-school humour can sometimes be very satisfying even if one is not present at the *dénouement*.

I shook hands all round; we were suddenly very shy of one another and could only say: 'Well, good-bye – take care of yourself, good-bye – good luck, and – well – good-bye.' I popped my head round the kitchen door to wave to Mrs Macbonn, who was pounding steak with brutal thoroughness, and she favoured me with a sort of reserved fascist salute, but her face muscles wouldn't run to a smile.

Joseph was taking me to the station as Jim was out in the car. I had already said good-bye to him, and received his renewed thanks for my part in his romance, which was now going swimmingly; he had bought Bessie a ring, and she even spoke of him as 'my fiancy in the motor business'.

The tin suitcase once more found a resting-place in the piggery, and, climbing up beside Joseph, I fell back on to the seat as he let in the clutch with a jerk, and we roared up the back drive and away from Chilford House for ever.

Chapter Twelve

When I got home I found it extremely difficult to resume my normal life again. Having been surrounded for so long by the atmosphere of domestic service I felt like a fish out of water, and even to sleep in a decent bed felt peculiar. I thought I might as well go on doing a bit of work while I was in the mood for it. I didn't want to get another job through 'Jobfinders' if it meant paying commission, but it was another matter when they rang me up and offered me 'casual labour'. I inquired very sheenily whether they wanted commission on it, and the woman at the other end evidently thought this in very bad taste, for she replied in a pinched voice, 'No, we do not,' and rang off.

She had offered me two jobs. The first was to cook and wait at a dinner for six people in a flat off Edgware Road. I got on to Mrs Drew, the prospective hostess, and she fluttered and stuttered at me through the telephone in a futile but amiable way.

'You must think it *very* stupid of me,' she said, 'but I simply don't know anything about cooking, and my maid suddenly has to go to her uncle's funeral, just on the day when I had planned this dinner. It's too late to put the guests off now, and I *do* so want it to be a tremendous success. Could you really manage the cooking and waiting by yourself?'

I said 'Yes' automatically, although I should have added, 'Not without a lot of chaos.'

'How *splendid*,' said Mrs Drew. 'I'll have everything ready for you. My maid is going to tell me what I should order before she goes. You will be sure to come in good time, won't you? What time will you get here?'

I asked her how much there would be to cook, and a lot of rustling went on at the other end, and she even dropped the telephone before she answered: 'Oh dear, I've gone and lost the list, but I think I can remember. Soup, I thought, to start with, or did I finally decide on grape-fruit? No, it was soup because I remember thinking "how warming". Grape-fruit is refreshing, of course, and rather party-like, too, don't you think? I wonder –'

'I should have grape-fruit,' I said decisively, thinking to save myself trouble.

'Do you think so? Very well then, let me just write that down. I'm afraid you'll think me very stupid, but my memory's so terrible. I simply can't remember what else I decided on. That list –'

'Well, shall I come along the day after tomorrow, at about half past four, and you can tell me then?' I said, as

I was getting sick of the ravings and gaspings that were coming over the air.

'Oh, yes, that will be *splendid*. The day after tomorrow then – half past four. *Splendid* – I do hope – ' She still didn't seem able to ring off, so I said, 'Good-bye' firmly and planked down my receiver.

The other job that the agency had offered me was to be a waitress at a cocktail party, which I understood was to be in the nature of a celebration for an engaged couple. I rang up Mrs Elkington, the mother of the bride-to-be, and she put on a suspicious voice and said she must see me before she engaged me, in case I was covered with sores or something, I suppose. The party was not for a week's time, but I thought I might as well get the inspection over at once, so I arranged to go along to her house near Sloane Square that afternoon. I decided that, to make a change and to pander to the finicky sound of Mrs Elkington's voice, I would be a very superior parlour-maid, deadly refined, and expecting to be addressed by my surname. I discarded Ye Olde Blacke Hatte for once and got myself up neat, plain, and prosperous, and it all seemed to go down quite well with Mrs Elkington.

She was sitting in her large drawing-room, surrounded by patterns of stuff, lists, and catalogues and all the para-phernalia that float about when a wedding is being arranged. I sat bolt upright on a chair rising out of a sea of tissue-paper, and told her that I had practically spent my life handing round trays.

'What is your name?' she inquired at the end of the interview.

'Plover, madam,' I answered, making a bad-smell-under-the-nose face.

She seemed quite impressed by this, so my hours of hunting through the telephone book had not been wasted.

'Do you wish me to wear mai black or mai blue, madam?'

'Black, please, with a cap, of course. Well, that's all, Plover, I shall expect you here on Tuesday at five o'clock then.'

As I was going down the stairs a very pretty dark girl passed me on her way up and raised her eyebrows at me in disinterested inquiry. She had a large diamond on her engagement finger, so I supposed she was the bride-to-be. She looked a bit sulky, and not particularly happy – perhaps it was a *mariage de convenance*.

Mrs Drew was my more immediate concern, however, so I ceased to be Plover and prepared to do battle in Edgware Road. I had not worn my uniform for some time, and I had forgotten just how dirty and weather-beaten it was. I retrieved it from where it was lying in a crimpled ball at the bottom of a drawer and ironed it and tried to sponge off some of the worst hall-marks of drudgery. I had had to cook in it when I was a 'general', covering the frills with a large gingham apron which I removed at the last minute so as to be able to transform myself from cook to parlour-maid when I had to take in the dishes.

I went along to Edgware Road in my blue as I wanted to keep the black to be Plover in. Mrs Drew was out when I arrived, but she had told the porter to let me in, and had left a long rambling note for me on the kitchen table. The menu for dinner was written out, interspersed with such remarks as: 'When the baker comes, please order one large white and one small brown or wholemeal if he has it, or currant ditto.' 'Do not use best butter. Marg. and lard in cupboard.' 'Can you stuff duck at both ends? If so, do.'

She had evidently changed her mind again about the grapefruit, for the dinner was to start with soup after all. Fried fish came next, with a shrimp sauce, and then the duck, with vegetables. 'Trifle,' said the list after that, 'with a dash of sherry, which is behind dustbin under sink.' I thought I had better make it at once if it was to get cold by dinner-time. Mrs Drew seemed to have bought the provisions more or less efficiently, though there was much too much of some things and not enough of others. Milk was rather short, so I had to make a stodgy trifle that was more sponge-cake than custard. I added quite a lot of the rather acid-smelling cooking sherry to pep it up a bit and put it into the refrigerator.

I was getting on quite nicely with the other things when Mrs Drew came to disturb my peace, staggering in under armfuls of flowers and parcels. She was an untidy little woman with wisps of hair escaping from under her hat, and only one glove.

'Dropped my other one in the shops somewhere,' she said; 'wasn't it stupid of me? I went back to look for it, but it was so difficult to remember where I'd been that, of course, I never found it. I think I've got everything now for the dinner – flowers, sweets, almonds. What's in this box, I wonder? I don't remember buying any biscuits or anything. Oh, no, of course, that must be my shoes.'

'Excuse me, madam,' I said, removing them from where she had laid them down on the fish.

'Thank you so much. Are you getting on all right, Miss – er? I shan't be in your way if I just arrange these flowers, shall I?'

It was not for me to say that I was in the middle of peeling vegetables in the sink, so I had to take them out and start on something else. For the next few minutes we bumped around together in the small kitchen, she chatting disjointedly about the dinner and me interjecting 'Pardon' or 'Excuse me' at intervals. After a bit I got tired of knocking into her and having to reach across or round her every time I wanted something out of the cupboard. I had heard enough to satisfy my curiosity about the people who were coming. The guests of honour, apparently, were her husband's boss and his wife, on whom Mrs Drew was desperately anxious to make an impression, and there was another married couple, a sister, thrown in to make weight. I went away to lay the table, and when I came back she had finished her flowers and was on her knees in front of the open oven, poking at the duck with a dubious finger. 'Which end did you stuff it?' she asked.

'You told me to stuff it both ends, madam,' I said righteously.

'Oh, did I? So I did. That's *splendid*. I do hope it's going to be enough for six people. What do you think?'

I didn't think it was nearly big enough myself, but there wasn't much point in adding to her anxiety by saying so, so I said, 'Ample, madam, excuse me,' and pushed her gently aside to baste the puny bird.

She went off at last to dress, and I started the familiar panic, suddenly realizing that, as usual, I had left myself too little time to get things done. Mrs Drew didn't help by flying in in her negligee to say: 'Oh dear, you've put out the white mats and I wanted the green. Didn't I tell you? Well, never mind. Or have you got time to change them?' I found it impossible to take things calmly with her flapping around, and soon we were both rushing about like a couple of clucking hens, working each other up into a state. Mr Drew came in in the middle of it all. He was a large, helpless sort of man, with a funny little baby face stuck up on top of his lumbering body, and a surprisingly thin high voice. His wife shooed him off to change, and after a bit he came into the kitchen with a half-bottle of sherry, just one grade higher than the stuff I had put into the trifle. He poured it out with great care into six glasses and carried them proudly into the drawing-room on a tray. I didn't know what they were going to drink at dinner – I had put wine glasses out on spec – so I went in to ask him if I was to open any bottles of anything.

'Here is the wine,' he said proudly, handing me a bottle of Empire Burgundy.

'You devils,' I thought, carrying it away at arm's length.

I took a pretty gloomy view of this dinner party altogether. The host and hostess were each as nervous and anxious as the other. He was pacing the floor fingering his tie, and she kept darting into the kitchen to ask futile questions. I took an even more gloomy view when I took out the trifle to see whether it had got properly cold. The thing was tepid! Even the dish was still faintly warm. I put my hand into the frig and, if anything, it was warmer in there than in the kitchen.

'Madam,' I said despairingly as Mrs Drew came poking in again in a trailing chiffon dress, 'your frig is out of order and the trifle hasn't got cold.'

'Oh, my goodness,' she gasped, 'didn't I tell you? It's been wrong for days and the man simply *will* not come. I keep ringing them up. Oh dear, oh dear, of course, it never occurred to me about the trifle, I thought you made it cold.'

'Well, madam, custard must be made hot, you know,' I pointed out, keeping my temper and my manners with difficulty.

'Yes, yes, of course. I never thought of that. How very dreadful it all is. Couldn't you put it out on the window-sill to cool?'

Well, it was her picnic, so I balanced it precariously on the narrow ledge and she went out, rather pleased with herself, but going into a terrified scuttle as the front-door bell rang.

I didn't imagine that the two people whom I admitted were the guests of honour, as they looked more like a pair of nervous ducks than anything else. I asked the sister whether she would like to go to the bedroom and she shook her head, after throwing a scared glance at her husband, who just stood with his toes turned in, making a pinched mouth of shyness. I opened the drawing-room door.

'Mr and Mrs Mottershead,' I announced, and shooed them firmly in.

The guests of honour were a little late, which was all to the good, as it gave the carrots a few more minutes in which to become less rock-like. When they did arrive I saw at once that they were not at all the sort of people to appreciate Empire wine and tepid trifle. 'Why have you come here in your fat opulence?' I wondered. Mr Garrow had probably been dragged here by his wife to fulfil some overdue politeness, and his red-veined face was sulky with annoyance as he followed his wife into the drawing-room.

'Dinner is served!' I announced afterwards, giving the carrots up as a bad job, and the embarrassed spasms of conversation broke off with relief as the party trooped into the dining-room with much shuffling of feet and 'After you's' at the door. After more shuffling they somehow all got seated, not at all in the places that Mrs Drew had intended, but she was not really clear about it in her mind anyway.

As usual, I was too busy to notice much of the social side of the dinner, but I could see that it was one of the saddest parties ever, and my food had turned out dreary and unappetizing, as if in sympathy with the general atmosphere. When I got as far as Mr Garrow with my reluctant chant of: 'Will you take wine?' he nearly had a stroke at the sight of the bottle. I think he thought that he would be offered something else, for I saw his eyes follow me incredulously as I filled up the last glass and went out to get my duck.

By the end of the next course Mr Garrow's conversation had dwindled from monosyllables to grunts, and his wife was struggling gallantly to keep it going. When it was time for the sweet my brain had gone as feathery as Mrs Drew's, and I couldn't for the life of me think what I had done with the trifle. It suddenly came back to me, and I fished it indoors, skimming off the black specks of soot as well as I could. Mr Garrow didn't miss much by refusing it. His eyes looked rather agonized, and I think his stomach was troubling him.

After coffee the ladies withdrew to talk about servants, and the gentlemen followed soon after as there was no port over which they could linger, and Mr Garrow's stomach was in no state to encourage jovial *camaraderie*. I was crashing away at the washing up when I heard someone come softly into the kitchen and close the door behind them. I hoped it was Mrs Drew with my pay, but when I turned round I was surprised to see Mr Garrow standing in a conspiratorial attitude with his finger to his lips.

'For God's sake,' he croaked, 'I must have a drink. Have you got anything?'

Poor man, he looked a wreck. Boredom and indigestion had played havoc with him. He was welcome to the remains of the cooking sherry, so I fished it out from behind the dustbin and, putting the bottle to his lips, he gulped it down at one draught. His eyebrows shot up as the stuff hit his stomach and his purple face became tinged with green.

'My God! What the devil –?' His stomach now told him it was time for him to leave, and leave hurriedly. He stumbled from the room, a broken man.

Plover was resurrected in a week's time, and, wearing her black, with hair scraped unbecomingly backwards, she trotted off to Mrs Elkington's. It was evidently going to be a large party, judging by the number of waitresses and barmen who were surging about in the basement. I was shown where to leave my coat, and put on the cap that I had bought for the occasion. I had made the great mistake of not trying it on at home, so I was not prepared for the awful vision that gazed at me from the mirror when I tied it round my head. A little farther back, perhaps, more like a halo and less of that visor effect – that was better. I was just going to powder my nose when I heard cries of: 'Where are all these girls? Rose, Lilian, Plover – where is this Plover?'

I popped out into the passage and met a fat, harassed butler with a list in his hand.

'Who are you?' he said.

'Ai'm Plover,' I replied, smoothing my apron.

'Oh, you're Plover, are you? I've been looking for you. Your job is to hand round trays of cocktails, which you'll collect at the bar, see? Walking through the two rooms and filling up same place. Right now you can carry some glasses up from that pantry there to the bar on the landing.'

I went into the pantry, where a maid with a face like a pig was loading glasses on to a tray.

'Ooh,' she said, 'did you know your cap was slipping off? Let me pull it down for you before you lose it.' She rushed at me, and before I could stop her had converted my halo into a visor again. I felt an awful fool, and knew I looked it, but I couldn't very well wear it the way I wanted if people were going to come and pull it forward all the time.

Finding a tray, I started to stack glasses on to it, and when it was full, carried it carefully upstairs, wondering what would happen in the not unlikely event of my dropping the whole lot. I arrived safely on the first floor landing, a large square expanse with buffet tables round three sides of it. Three or four waiters were making champagne cocktails as fast as they could go, and I longed for one. I wouldn't have minded a *marron glacé* either; a huge bowl of them was right under my nose as I unloaded my glasses at one end of the bar, and I could easily have pinched one without anybody seeing, but 'No,' I said to myself, 'Plover would never do a thing like that.' Would Plover be above making friends with one of the barmen so that he would save her a cocktail when the party was over? I thought she might descend to it in her off moments, so I smiled seductively at the nearest one, a thin, pale youth with a protuberant Adam's apple. He stared through me unseeingly, so I tried again, and this time he just gave me a brief smile for civility's sake – a mere twitch of the lips. Poor Plover, spurned and humiliated! I hadn't realized that I looked quite so frightful in that cap. I pushed it up a bit surreptitiously as I went downstairs, but it had fallen over my eyes again by the time I got back to the pantry, so the pig-girl had nothing to complain of. I pushed it up again when she went out, but it was no good. I would have to put up with looking like a 1920 tennis player and give up the idea of a cocktail.

I carried up two more trayloads, and then somebody told me to get some cocktails and take my place in one of the two big reception rooms leading out of each other, as the guests were due to arrive at any minute. The family were already standing uneasily about in new dresses and wondering whether they had invited people for the right day. I thought they looked as if they needed a drink, so I advanced carefully towards them over the parquet with my tray. Mrs Elkington was looking queenly in blue velvet with an excess of orchids.

'Have I time for a drink I wonder before we have to start receiving people? Why don't you have one, John? You look as if you needed it.'

John, I supposed, was her husband, a nondescript, nervous little man. He had to clear his throat twice before he could start to answer.

Their daughter, the girl I had met the other day on the

stairs, broke in: 'Well, I'm going to have one, I feel terrible. How about you, Aunt Madge?' I gave her and Aunt Madge a cocktail and Uncle somebody thought it was a good idea, too. I looked round for the fiancé, but there was nobody in the room that I'd have had for any money. He couldn't have come yet, unless – oh dear, *could* it be this square little turkey-cock with red hair, who was even now making free with his arm about the lovely girl's waist? No wonder she felt terrible and looked sulky – who wouldn't? I grudgingly offered him a drink, and he took it in a pink and podgy hand. I couldn't think what to do now, so I copied one or two of the other wait-resses and took up my stand by the wall, wearing an impersonal face. The fat butler appeared from the landing and said: 'The first guests are arriving, madam.'

Mother, father, daughter, and fiancé ranged themselves by the door, and in a minute or two the butler started to announce people in a quite unnecessarily loud voice.

'Mrs Boggan and Miss Kathleen Boggan!' he yelled, and two rather dusty-looking people shuffled in and were greeted effusively, though it was obvious that nobody knew who they were. The Boggans were well in advance of the main body of the guests, and they looked as if they wanted to go home again, but Aunt Madge and I came to the rescue simultaneously, I with my drink and she with her mauve hair and much-lifted face. She chatted to them about nothing in particular, and after a bit people started to arrive thick and fast. There was soon quite a crowd in the rooms, and I was rather scared of venturing among them with my tray, but one of the waitresses passed by me and said: 'You got to circulate, see?'

I had to leave my wall and pick my way carefully through the crowd, offering drinks here and there, and feeling as if I ought to be crying, 'Chocolates! Cigarettes!' I loaded on some more cocktails at the bar and started off all over again. It was really very amusing hearing snatches of conversation and observing people from under my cap, which was well down over my eyes by now.

'My dear, have you *ever*?' I heard one smart deb say to another. 'That horrid little man. How Ann *could* have –'

'I know; it can't be love. If you ask me it's a question of anything to get away from that mother of hers. They fight like hell, you know.' I wanted to hear more, but a large male was clicking his fingers at me a few yards away, so I had to go and give him and his lady-friend a drink. She gazed up at him with adoring eyes as he handed it her with an air.

'Oh, *thank* you,' she said as if he had bought it for her. 'Thank me, not him, he ain't done anything,' I thought as I moved away.

I was doing good work. My cocktails went rapidly, and I had to go back to the bar for more before I had got through the two rooms. I didn't know what to do with the dirty glasses that I had collected on my way. I asked a woman who was standing on the stairs directing people to the cloak-room, and she said: 'Couldn't say, I'm sure. Ladies' cloak-room, madam? Up the stairs and first on the right, if you please.' They didn't want them at the bar and I obviously couldn't carry them down the stairs as guests were still flowing steadily up.

I felt a bit lost; I didn't like to ask the barman who had turned me down, so I tried the next one along, who was bald and kind-looking. He jerked a thumb towards a small door leading out of the hall that I hadn't noticed before. I went through it and nearly fell down a long flight of stairs on the other side. One glass shot off the tray and bumped to the bottom where it broke with a noise like a plate-glass window.

'Struth, who done that?' said a raucous voice from below, and a creature in a green baize apron appeared, shook his head at me reprovingly, and vanished, leaving me to pick up the pieces. I kicked them into a corner, and was just wondering where to go now when Green Baize reappeared from a sort of scullery where he was evidently washing up.

'*In* 'ere, butter-fingers,' he said, and I dumped down my tray hurriedly and fled back up the stairs. I didn't wish to linger in his scullery as I felt he had me at a disadvantage, not to mention the fact that garlic had figured on his luncheon menu.

I loaded my tray at the bar again and set off on my circuit. Three more rounds and my feet were drawing as never before, but there was still quite a crowd left, so it was no good their telling me that they wanted to have the weight taken off them. It was tiring work and I began to feel a bit dazed and forgot to be Plover all the time. I offered a drink to two men who were talking together, and when one said to the other, 'What station does one go from for Portsmouth?' I answered automatically, 'Waterloo.' I was horrified, and they were a little startled, but being perfect gentlemen they smiled politely and said, 'Thank you.'

I pulled myself together after this *faux pas* and dashed about alertly, spilling some drink down a woman's back in my excess of zeal. She never noticed, so I hurried away before some kind friend could point it out.

The guests were beginning to thin out, but there were still quite a few who looked as if they would be with us for some time yet. I really felt exhausted, so next time I passed the little door I popped through it and knocked back two cocktails off my tray without drawing breath. I emerged a new woman, beamingly impervious to the suspicious glance that the bald barman gave me.

'To hell with Plover and her scruples!' I thought, deftly taking a *marron glacé* as I passed, without checking my stride.

There were not many people left now and they all

seemed to have drinks, so I leaned against a wall and watched them, feeling quite mellow. Ann Elkington was sitting on a sofa having an intimate conversation with someone who was certainly not her fiancé. He was strutting about at the other end of the room, talking business to an elderly bore. Mrs Elkington was having a good gossip with a woman who nodded the ostrich feathers in her hat every time they came to a bit of scandal. The host had disappeared. As one who had also been present since the beginning, I didn't blame him. I stood on like Casabianca, and some of the people trickled away, till there were only one or two groups left. A voice at my elbow roused me from the coma into which I had sunk. It was the girl who had told me to circulate. She thought me rather a poor fish and said pityingly: 'Don't you know you can go now? There's eats in the kitchen.'

I realized how hungry I was, so I threw my tray down on the bar and ran down the back stairs. I heard a lot of voices coming from the end of a passage, so I went along and there was the entire company with their mouths full of left-over sandwiches and cake. I suddenly felt fearfully shy. It may have been my imagination, but I sensed a rather hostile atmosphere. Nobody had been at all pally all the evening; Plover was hungry, but she was not popular. I spotted Green Baize, and the undesirous barman, and the pig-girl saw me in the doorway and shot a scornful glance at my head. I definitely couldn't face it, so I crept away to the room where I had left my coat and saw that my cap was sitting rather drunkenly over one eye. However, shy or not shy, I was not going without my money. Luckily the fat butler came out into the passage, so I didn't have to go into the kitchen.

'Who are *you*?' he said as I accosted him.

'I'm still Plover and I want my money,' I said, tired and cross.

'All right, all right, all right,' he said, drawing ten shillings out of his pocket in a lordly way and handing it to me with the tips of his fingers.

'Good naight!' I said, rallying Plover just once more before letting her pass into the valley of the shadow as I passed out of the back door into the area.

Chapter Thirteen

I frittered away another month or two doing occasional cooking and waiting jobs, but there didn't seem to be much demand for me in this capacity. Odd jobs like this, of course, are paid proportionately much higher than a regular place, and I suppose people thought they weren't getting their money's worth in me. The only person who ever engaged me more than once was a sour old lady, who was willing to pay me three-and-six a time to go and cook her dinner three evenings a week. After one or two treks out to her flat somewhere beyond the Crystal Palace I decided it wasn't worth it, and in any case she was becoming sourer and sourer as she got to know me better. I sat around at home and waited for the telephone to ring, but there was not much doing. In the absence of more high-class jobs I even went out once as a scullery-maid to wash up after a dinner party – a sordid pastime that turned out to be unexpectedly comic.

I was dumped into the scullery the moment I arrived, with strict injunctions not to stir from the sink. Starting with cocktail glasses, I ploughed my way through the mountains of stuff that were hurled at me by a procession of cheerfully indifferent maids as the dinner upstairs progressed. I was to do it all apparently. No one else intended to have any truck with dishcloths and greasy water – they had other plans for the evening. I gathered from the odd word thrown at me as they crashed in and out that the people upstairs were all going off to a dance at about ten o'clock.

After about two hours' slavery at the sink, with the skin on my hands becoming wrinkled and decayed-looking from the hot water, I heard attractive sounds of revelry floating down the passage from the kitchen. The noise grew louder, the blare of wireless mingling with shrieks and screams of high-pitched laughter. Although I had been told not to leave my sink, I wasn't going to be left out of it any longer. I had almost finished my work, anyway, so I threw down my sodden dishcloth and went along to gate-crash the most wonderful party that was being held in the kitchen. The butler, a sporting old devil with white hair, was taking advantage of his possession of the wine cellar key to celebrate his birthday in the best champagne and port that the house could offer. There he sat, jigging one of the parlour-maids on his knee to the tune of the foxtrot that some of the others were dancing.

'Heh!' he roared at me as I appeared in the doorway, 'what d'you think you're doing in here?'

'I've finished. Can I have a drink?' I roared back, emboldened by the gaiety of the atmosphere.

'Make yourself at home, this is Liberty 'All!' he shouted, and the boot-boy handed me a glass of champagne and said would I like to swing it with him. We swung it. We sang, we danced, we drank, we bumped into people, and played slap-and-tickle with everyone. They were a delightful lot in that kitchen, even if it was at somebody else's expense. The master of the house was a rich man anyway and could well afford it. I'm sure it was a much better party than any he had ever given upstairs for his debutante daughter, with inane girls and callow youths vying with each other to see who could enjoy themselves least.

I left before the end. I was doing fine with the boot-boy, but I suddenly felt very peculiar and thought I had better take the mixture of port and champagne home and put it to bed. A scullery-maid doesn't usually go home from her drudgery in a taxi, but this one had to. It was not until I was in bed, and hovering above the black abyss of alcholic oblivion, that I remembered that I had never finished my washing-up. Anyway, I hadn't had my pay either, but I just didn't care.

Apart from this one lively incident my jobs in various houses only served to convince me that human nature is not all it might be. I must have struck it unlucky, for apart from the fact that most of the people I went to never wanted to see me again, one meeting was certainly enough for me. I suppose I happened to go to poisonous people because they were the sort whom no maid would stand for long. I was beginning to take a gloomy view of life, but one evening I went out to cook a dinner and discovered that there was hope for the world yet.

Everything went right that evening, it was most peculiar. The egg that I put into the soup didn't curdle it, the omelettes were neat outside and runny inside, the meat was tender, and the fried potatoes crisp. Strangest of all, the cheese *soufflé* was ready at exactly the right moment. I hadn't dropped or spilled anything when handing round, nor had I gashed or burned myself in my usual style.

I was standing in the kitchen after dinner, pinching myself to see if it wasn't all a dream. I had just come to the conclusion that it was either something to do with the stars, or else my guardian angel had decided to throw his weight about, when the mistress of the house came in.

Mrs Vaughan had grown-up children – one of them was there that evening – but her hair had refused to go white or her figure to spread. She was like a brisk little sparrow, always hopping about doing things. She had even kept jumping up at dinner to get things instead of mouthing at me, like most of my employers. Her motto was, evidently, 'If you want a thing done, do it yourself' –

that was probably the way she kept her figure. She pottered round the kitchen, fiddling with things while she talked.

'Miss Dickens,' she said, breathing on a glass and polishing it with her handkerchief, 'we did so enjoy your dinner tonight. Everything went off wonderfully, I thought. I suppose you wouldn't ever – ? No, I don't suppose you would – well, I don't see why not after all, it's worth asking you, anyway. I've been wondering if you could possibly help us out. Would you consider coming here as a permanency? – As cook-general, I mean? I have a girl who comes in for housework in the mornings, but apart from that we're stranded. My cook walked out suddenly – she was mad anyway, poor thing – and I can't get anyone for love or money. It's not a large flat, as you can see. The work's not hard, it's just my husband and me when there's no one staying. We never have formal parties or anything, people come into meals quite a lot, of course, and I really think you might be happy here. I'm sure we should be more than happy to have you.'

The idea attracted me, they seemed such very nice people, so I accepted as soon as I could get a word in edgeways. I felt I ought to tell her that my performance tonight had been well above my usual standard, but I didn't get a chance, because the flow of speech had started once more, and the whole thing was fixed up with scarcely a word from me. She tried to persuade me to live in, because she thought it would be less tiring for me, but I didn't want to risk any more black iron beds or smelly furniture, so I produced the widowed mother again as an excuse for sleeping at home.

It wasn't far to go in the morning, and as they didn't want to be called particularly early I didn't have to rise at crack of dawn.

I made early-morning tea, and, going into the bedroom, dumped it down between the two mounds of sleeping humanity. Mrs Vaughan woke as I drew the curtains and plunged in the most amazing way straight from sleep into conversation. All about the breakfast it was, and where I should find this and where to put that. I had a feeling she had told it me all the night before, but my brain, which had been conscious for a good hour longer than hers, wasn't nearly as awake. Thoughts were clicking around in Mrs Vaughan's mind with whirling speed, but in mine they were still groping about in a confused fog left over from the hours of darkness.

She looked rather sweet in bed, very tiny, with a wee pigtail of thin hair lying neatly over one shoulder. I stood looking at her with my mouth open, taking in some of the talk, and eventually the larger hump in the other bed heaved and said: 'Really, dearest, what a noise you make.'

'Well, I must tell Monica what to do, it's her first morning. If you'd be a little more helpful and say whether you want sardines for breakfast we might get somewhere.'

'Sardines?' he said on a huge yawn. 'Not if they're like the last lot you gave me.'

'Don't be silly,' said his wife, 'those were the ones Agnes opened and left in the tin for two weeks. They've been thrown away days ago – I hope. I had the most amazing dream last night, all about Uncle Rupert. We were in Prague –' Bird-like, her brain skipped from one subject to the next with bewildering quickness. I was still standing with my mouth open in case there were any more instructions, so I coughed to show I was still there.

'Oh, yes, Monica, sardines,' she said, hopping from Uncle Rupert to breakfast with the same agility. 'And scrambled egg!' she called after me as I went out. '– So I knelt down in the road,' she had picked up the threads again before I was out of the door.

I started to dust the dining-room, but it was a disheartening task as there were so many things standing about. Framed photographs there were and ornaments and statues of every description, probably presents that couldn't be thrown away in case the person who gave them should die. I contented myself with flicking a feather duster over one or two things, including a few small silver cups for seaside golf tournaments. It was obviously hopeless to embark on pictures on the walls, there were so many of them that I could hardly see the colour of the wall-paper. When I heard Mr Vaughan go slop-slopping to his bath I laid the table and started to cook the breakfast.

Mrs Vaughan came soon pattering in in her little red slippers to see how I was getting on.

'Are you sure there's nothing I can do to help you?' she asked. 'I know it's difficult the first morning. Here, let me take this coffee-pot in for you.' It wasn't ready to go in yet as it hadn't any coffee in it, but I let her trot away with it and went and retrieved it when she had gone back to her room to dress. Mr Vaughan was ready before I was, and prowled about, saying, 'Why isn't breakfast in? I shall be late for the office.'

'Now, darling, you know we never have it before a quarter past nine,' said his wife, popping out of her room with her mouth full of hairpins and her hands busy with her small bun. 'You never leave the house before ten anyway, so don't pretend you're so hard-working.'

'I thought of walking across the park this morning. I want to see what our wonderful bureaucratic system is doing about those trenches.'

'Well, you can see tomorrow. I don't suppose they'll have done anything before then. I've told you ten times it's Monica's first morning so don't be difficult. She's doing very well; I think she'll do.'

I kept the kitchen door open to listen to their idle chatter as I finished getting the breakfast ready. I was glad to see that there was going to be no *pas devant la bonne* in this household; they either considered me so human that I was almost one of them, or so stupid that I couldn't take much in.

While they were having their breakfast there was a ring at the back door and I opened it on a large girl of greasy but cheerful aspect. She goggled at me and could have been knocked down by the proverbial feather.

'Where's Agnes?'

'She's gone. I'm the new cook.'

'Go on, you don't say. Things certainly move fast around here. One day I come and there's Agnes, and the next day I come and "Agnes is gone", says you. What's your name, dear?'

'Monica.'

'That's ever so nice, I like that. Mine's Maud. That's pretty, too, I think. Mrs Vaughan says there's a poem about me. Fancy! Ever such a nice lady, Mrs Vaughan is. A great one for a chat, too. No swank, though she does know her place, if you know what I mean. Not above sitting down to a boiled egg now and then when she's alone. Got a cup of tea for me, dear? Agnes and me, we always used to have a cup of tea before starting on the trivial round, the common task, as we say Sundays.'

Anyone could have got on with Maud, she was such a cheery soul, and we were bosom pals by the time we had finished the second cup.

'Fortunes now,' she said, turning both our cups upside down and tapping on their bottoms with a mystic rhythm. 'Let's see what you got. Oh, you lucky girl! Look, dear, you got two spoons near the top. That means flirtations, and this ring by the handle, that's a wedding. That's a lovely cup, that is. Look at all these dots. They mean money coming to you.'

I was thrilled to the core. 'How d'you do it, Maud?' I asked.

'Oh, it's a science, dear, same as astronomy and that. Oh, look!' she said, turning up her cup, 'scissors. That's quarrels. All the leaves at the bottom, too, that means bad luck. I'm afraid you couldn't possibly call this a swan here, could you? I sail into more prosperous waters if it is. I never seem to have much luck with the cups. Cards, now, that's another story, but cups! The things I've seen! I had a coffin once. That was a terrible day.'

'Did anyone die?'

'No, dear, but they might have. You've got to think of that.'

The front door slammed. 'Ah, that's our boss off to work, bless his heart. Her ladyship'll be in directly, to order, so we'd better be getting a move on.' She explained to me how the work was supposed to be divided between us, and then Mrs Vaughan came in and told it me all over again. She and Maud were evidently old friends. They had a little chat about Maud's mother's diabetes, before she went off to make beds, and Mrs Vaughan settled down to order the food. She kept dashing out to answer the telephone, which I thought rather complicated things, but she seemed to be able to cope all right.

'Steak, tonight,' she would be saying. Ting-ting, ting-ting! went the telephone, and off she would run. She reappeared saying: 'with plenty of onions,' as if she had never been away. We got everything settled and she walked out for good, only to reappear two minutes later to say that someone had rung up and asked themselves to lunch. While we were in the middle of rearranging things slightly, the milkman arrived.

'How's your little boy getting on, Mr Finnigan?' she asked.

'Nicely, thank you, Mum. They say he can come out in a week. It was ever so good of you to send them toys. Thank you ever so much, I'm sure.'

Mrs Vaughan went off to spend the morning at a prison, handing out library books to the convicts. The woman was nothing but a communal benefactress, and I was not surprised when the lunch visitor turned out to be a woman who had left her husband and wanted advice, and, incidentally, money. She got both, from what I could hear as I handed round the cutlets and treacle tart. I was the parlour-maid, Maud only did housework and 'rough', and she left before lunch. She fulfilled the duties of a char really, though the word didn't fit her. She had another cup of tea 'for the road', and saw a lighthouse in it, which sent her off in good spirits, babbling of legacies.

One of Mrs Vaughan's two married daughters dropped in to tea, a stout, overpowering girl, about three times the size of her mother. They were discussing some rather absorbing medical details when I took in the tea, and I wanted to hear more, so I listened outside the door.

'Oh, dear, she's forgotten the sugar,' I heard Mrs Vaughan say. 'No, don't ring, Frances, we must save her legs. She has enough to do as it is. Let's do without sugar, I don't really mind whether I have it or not, do you?'

'Oh, Mummy, you know I can't drink tea without it. I suppose I'll have to get it myself. Really, you and your maids, the place might be a charitable institution. You collect a lot of old crocks and pay them colossal wages, and then proceed to spoil them, which they probably don't appreciate at all. I hope this one's not quite such an imbecile as Agnes. She –' Here I surprised them by walking haughtily in with the sugar basin. I placed it on the tray, and stalked out again in my best Plover manner. Imbecile indeed! Old crock! I'd show her. They should realize that I had known better days in high-class kitchens.

For a little while I strove to be the perfect maid, nearly bursting myself with efficiency and correctness, but it wore off after a few days. Mrs Vaughan was just as charming to me whether I made Nonsenses or not, and the lack of formality with which all sorts of odd people tumbled over one another in the flat didn't encourage me to waste valuable energy on punctiliousness. There was a family dinner party while I was still conducting my efficiency campaign, and I couldn't make out why Clare, the youngest daughter, was reaching all round the table, opening the mustard and pepper pots.

'Look, everybody!' she cried, 'a revolution in the Vaughan household! Mustard and pepper in all the pots!' I didn't see what was funny enough in that to produce screams of joyous laughter from everyone.

'Look, Pa, that's something you've never known before isn't it?'

'I've told your mother time and again –' he began, but nobody paid any attention.

'We've been used to shaking pepper pots fruitlessly for so long that you make us feel peculiar,' explained Clare to me as I handed her the bread sauce. I liked her. She was completely naive and friendly, like a child, though she had one of her own, 'turned three', according to Maud. Frances was a bit more uppish, and I don't think her husband liked her particularly. He had probably married her on account of her father. He was in his office, so had hopes of advancement, but apart from that he thought Mr Vaughan quite the most entertaining man that ever walked. He was a wonderful audience for him, and would go black in the face and have to be led from the room if his father-in-law so much as said, 'Pass the salt.'

Although Maud was only thirty, she had been working for the family since she was eighteen, and knew more about their characters and life histories than they did themselves. I had a lot from Mrs Vaughan, of course, who was always ready for a chat at any hour of the day or night, and what she didn't tell me Maud supplied, with great exaggeration of detail. Once or twice a week, if there was a lot of work to be done, or a room to be turned out, she would stay a bit longer and have lunch with me in the kitchen. On these days, Mrs Vaughan, who always did us proud in the way of food, would order something for which she knew Maud had a particular fancy. Pork was her special delight. It made her face shine more than ever. Mrs Vaughan never poked into the larder, or inquired after puddings and things that had appeared once in the dining-room and only been half finished. They hardly ever appeared again if Maud and I could help it. 'Pity to leave it in the larder to go off,' we would say, as we polished off the best part of a trifle or blackcurrant tart. I got revoltingly fat under Maud's influence and nearly burst out of my uniform.

After lunch, she would relax with a long sigh and proceed to regale me with titbits and anecdotes about our employers. She was surprisingly old-fashioned in that she had quite a feudal feeling for the family. She was passionately keen that they should be kept in their place, both through our unfailing efforts and their own. She even thought that Mrs Vaughan 'demeaned herself' a bit too much, and certainly no one else might go as far.

'It's not *right*, Monica,' she would say. 'Mrs Chesterton' (that was Clare) 'didn't ought to walk about the streets without a hat – gives people ideas. But she always was one for doing funny things. D'you know –' in an awestruck whisper, 'she has no white curtains up in any of the windows of her house! Very strange, I call that. It's not right, you know, for a young lady not to have everything nice. I used to tell her fortune with the cards before she got married. A tall, dark man, she was going to meet. Well, Mr Chesterton's fair, but he's tall all right, so it just shows. Ever such a nice gentleman he is. Always gives you your name.'

I was at the sink, washing dishes to the accompaniment of Maud's voice. 'What's the time?' I called over my shoulder.

'Half past kissing time, time to kiss again,' said Maud infuriatingly, as I really wanted to know. There was to be a tea party for the children this afternoon, and I had a lot to do. It turned out to be nearly half past three.

'Oh, my Gordon!' said Maud. 'I ought to be gone

hours ago, Mother'll be getting nervy. You keep me here, chatting –'

'And I've got to start making cakes and things,' I said, breaking a plate in my haste. Maud got up and picked up a cloth.

'Come on, dear, I'll dry for you.'

'Oh, Maud, you are a love. Thanks ever so. Oh, heavens, I've hardly got any flour, I'll have to go and ring up for some. What a life this is.'

'Cheer up, dear, soon be dead,' said Maud blithely, breaking another plate, and hurling the pieces into the rubbish bin with gay abandon.

I went into the drawing-room where Mrs Vaughan was writing letters.

'May I use the phone, madam? I've run out of flour.'

'Certainly, Monica. Can you manage? I'll do it for you if you like. Did I hear Maud? She ought to have gone hours ago. She never used to stay so long when Agnes was here. She was frightened of her. She –'

I had to interrupt her, as a voice was saying, 'Hullo?' so her narrative was suspended while I put the fear of God into the grocer and made him promise to send round at once.

'She was a little mad, you know,' went on Mrs Vaughan, as soon as I put down the receiver. 'One day, we were going to have a dinner party, and I went into the kitchen about something, and there was Agnes sitting under the table, waving a burning duster, and singing "God Save the King". It *was* Coronation year, but still. She was a dear old thing, really though – '

I had to stand there listening politely, though there were masses of things I wanted to be doing. Mrs Vaughan talked and wrote at the same time, so she couldn't see me fidgeting pointedly, and edging towards the door. Luckily the telephone rang, and though it was only a wrong number, it gave me a chance to escape.

When Maud had finished the drying, she heaved off to Paddington Green, where she lived with the diabetic one. Frances and her two children arrived early, only a few minutes after the grocer's boy, so I had to leave my scones to open the door to them.

'Ooh, look!' piped the eldest, a fat little brute called Angeline. 'She's got white stuff all over her face. Why has she, Mummy? She does look funny. Mummy, Mummy, doesn't she look funny?'

'Hush, dear,' said Frances, throwing me a surprised look. I had been prepared to undress the children, but I took umbrage and removed my flour-streaked face to the kitchen.

I made a lot of tea cakes and scones, and little buns, and I had made a big iced cake the day before, rather damp and undercooked, and probably fatal to small insides, but that was the mothers' lookout. I took everything into the drawing-room, where Mrs Vaughan was crawling on the floor playing bears with her three grandchildren. One or two nieces had also arrived with their young, and the place was in an uproar. To the children's great delight, and her own unconcern, Mrs Vaughan's bun had lost its moorings. I looked round for somewhere to put the heavy tray.

'Oh dear,' said my mistress, coming out from under the piano, 'I think we'd better have tea in the diningroom, then we can all sit round the table.'

Out I staggered, and bustled about finding tablecloths and extra chairs, and by the time everything was ready the tea was getting cold. I was glad I hadn't bothered to make a fresh pot, for the grown-ups didn't notice. Each mother was too intent on watching her own children, with tears of pride in her eyes, as they slopped their milk and spat out masticated gobs of bread and jam on the clean tablecloth.

Clare's little boy was my favourite, and she brought him into the kitchen after tea. I left him cold, but he felt a social obligation to entertain me, so went through his repertoire of songs with the air of one pandering to an inferior mentality.

Mr Vaughan came home before they had gone, and pretty soon he was on his knees too, and the whole flat was in such a turmoil that I couldn't even get among them to clear the tea. Screams and yells of over-excitement rent the air, and Philip, Frances' son who was a minute edition of his father, was, like him, convulsed with laughter at the ponderous antics of his grandfather. Needless to say, this turned into hysteria, and he lay kicking on his back till his mother came and took him off under one arm.

'Really, Pa, you are a nuisance,' she said irritably, 'you always work him up so. I'm going to take him home before he chokes himself or something. He'll probably be sick when we get back, anyway. Where on earth's Angeline got to?'

'Don't fuss, Frances,' said Mrs Vaughan, arriving on the scene with the other child. 'I've been wondering whether perhaps Angy's getting too much starch. Look at her little tum, it's like a football.' She prodded the offending part, and Angeline began to add her yells to her brother's. The exasperated Frances said hasty good-byes, and removed them both. Their yells could be heard floating up the lift-shaft as they descended.

When the last child had been hauled and slapped out of the front door by its harassed nurse or mother, Mrs Vaughan sank with a sigh of relief on to the sofa in the drawing-room, where I was tidying up.

'Thank goodness we're alone tonight,' she said to no one in particular. 'I'm really dead tired. Oh, that tele-phone!' She jumped up, though I was much nearer it than she was. I had ceased to bother about answering it when it rang, as she always came running anyway, and stood by my side saying, 'Is it for me?' while I was saying, 'Yes, madam; hold the line, madam.' It generally was for her, but even if someone did happen to want her husband, it made no difference. She carried on a long conversation with them in his place, until they sometimes forgot what they had rung up about, and rang off before she had even fetched Mr Vaughan.

'Hullo!' she was saying now. 'Oh, *hullo*, my dear – to-night? But, of course, we always love to see you. Sweet of you to want to come. Quarter to eight? – all right, that'll be lovely. Good-bye. There!' she said, turning to me, 'I spoke too soon. Mr and Mrs Fleming want to come to dinner tonight. I couldn't say no. I always think it's so touching when the young people want to come to the older ones. I hope there's enough to eat, that's all. What were we going to have?'

'Wild duck, madam.'

'Oh, dear, that won't be enough for four. We'd better have tomorrow's joint, and the duck can keep. If we've got enough vegetables, that'll be all right, and perhaps you could do us a Scotch woodcock or something, for a savoury.'

'Yes, madam. I'll go and put the joint in the oven, madam.' I spoke glumly, and I certainly felt glum. I still had all the washing up from tea to do, and then a dinner for four on top of that – my head ached from the racket of the afternoon, and my legs were not themselves at all. Anyway, I thought, I would leave most of the clearing up of the children's mess – sticky fingermarks on doors and paint, and bits of broken toys under the furniture. Maud and I could do it tomorrow. I banged out of the room, and Mrs Vaughan put me to shame by rushing after me saying: 'You poor dear, I'm afraid you're having a dreadful lot to do today. I tell you what, I'll help you with the washing up of the tea things. That'll make a little difference, won't it?'

Mr Vaughan came out of the dining-room. 'Monica! I wish you'd clear this table, I want to use it.'

'Oh, John,' said his wife, 'you're not going to work now, surely?'

'No, of course not. What d'you take me for? I'm going to paste photographs in the album.'

'Well, you must let Monica lay the table when she wants to. Mary and George are coming to dinner.'

'Oh, dearest, I thought we were alone. I wanted to listen to the wireless. There's a good concert from Stuttgart. *Why* must you always ask people? Mary's so affected, she gives me the shivers.'

'She isn't, John; she's perfectly sweet. She's probably frightened of you. Some people are, you know, goodness knows why. Anyway, I didn't ask them, they asked themselves.'

'Well, it's a bore just the same. I think I'll have a Pink

Gin to cheer me up.' There was a pause, followed by a roar: 'Who's taken the key of the wine cupboard?'

I had been clearing the table in the dining-room while all this was going on in the hall, and I came out now with my tray, as Mrs Vaughan pointed out that the key was in the cupboard door. 'Well, that's not its place,' he growled. 'It's supposed to live in the drawer of the hall table.'

'But, darling, that's so silly. If the idea is to stop Monica and me from drinking ourselves to death on your old brandy, there's no point in hiding the key where we know where it is. Why not either secrete it on your person, or else leave it in the door, which saves a lot of trouble. You're a sweet old man.' He screwed up his face to receive her kiss, patted her on the shoulder, and ambled off quite happily into the dining-room with his photos. He didn't seem to mind at all that no one took him seriously. I had been scared stiff at first when he shouted at me for forgetting things or leaving the lights on, but I was already coming to regard him with the same affectionate lack of awe as the rest of the family.

Mrs Vaughan followed me into the kitchen, where I was just putting the joint into the oven. I started the washing up, and she stood by me and dried, pausing at intervals to go off into a soliloquy about something that she was wiping.

'I always think this is such a dear little milk jug. It was

my mother's, you know; she loved silver just like I do. Oh, dear, this plate's got rather a bad crack. I expect that was Agnes. You will be very careful of it, won't you? Perhaps we oughtn't to use it. It's the only one left out of six that we had as a wedding present.'

We were getting along quite nicely, though there was still a lot to be done, when the front-door bell rang.

'I'll go,' said Mrs Vaughan. 'Your hands are wet.' I heard her greeting somebody in the hall: 'Why, Miss Nitchin! How nice to see you! Come in and have a glass of sherry.' She took the visitor into the drawing-room, and came flying back to me.

'I'm so sorry, Monica, I wanted to help you. Poor Miss Nitchin has so few friends. I simply must talk to her for a little. I only hope she won't expect to be asked to dinner. Would you bring in the sherry and some glasses?'

I was annoyed, not with her, because she was so charming and considerate, but with life in general. Fatigue, I suppose, because really, when I thought about it, I had no grievance at all. I told myself sourly that I was unworthy of such a good mistress, but it didn't stop me taking a very jaundiced view of Miss Nitchin, who sat shabbily and diffidently on the sofa sipping sherry, and moaning about the slump in the dressmaking business. She infuriated me to the point of almost cutting off the top of my thumb, as I sliced carrots viciously, wishing they were Miss Nitchin. I found some plaster in the bathroom, and got on with my cooking as well as I could. I decided to leave the rest of the washing up till after dinner. When I wanted to lay the table, I went and stood pointedly in the dining-room doorway, but it made no impression on the hunched figure sitting within, absorbed with pots of paste and snapshots of the back view of his wife as a foreground to the Grand Canal. I tried walking round the table and tripping over the cord of his electric lamp, and jogging his elbow at a ticklish moment. This did the trick.

'Oh, God,' he said, getting up resignedly, 'is there no peace?' I helped him gather up his things, and he took himself off to the drawing-room, where he luckily solved the Nitchin problem by saying: 'Oh, hullo, Miss Nitchin! Just going? That's too bad.'

This blasted her hopes of staying to dinner, and she went off, still moaning, only about ten minutes before the Flemings arrived. Mr Vaughan was right about the affectation. Mary Fleming spent most of the evening giggling and chirruping coyly at him. He was very nice to her, however, and she sat on his right hand, and before long he was discovering how pretty she was, and feeling quite a gay old dog. His wife noticed my bandaged thumb, while I was handing round the dishes, and showed great concern. 'I'll put some iodine on it for you afterwards. Now don't forget and go home before I've seen it.'

There was not much chance of my forgetting it, as it was giving me real agony. Between my thumb, and my head and my legs, the end of dinner found me a wreck; I felt more like putting my head in the gas oven, than clearing the table and washing up. My eye fell on a decanter of sherry which was standing on the sideboard, and I considered it fixedly for some time. Well, after all, why shouldn't I? One quick nip – it would just give me enough heart to finish off what I had to do. Glancing furtively over my shoulder, I poured out quite half a tumblerful, and tossed it off. Everything went black, and then balls of fire shot up my throat, and exploded in a thousand stars before my eyes. It was not sherry at all – it was whisky! Once I had got over the first shock, I felt terrific. I reeled into the kitchen, polished off the work with the speed of a machine, and rushed off home, quite forgetting the iodine, for the pain in my thumb was miraculously cured.

Chapter Fourteen

One day, after I had been at the Vaughans' about a month, the peace of an October Sunday afternoon was broken by a violent pealing of the bell, and hammerings of fists on the front door. I left the crumpets, which I had just put under the grill, and flew to open it. A distraught figure there – Clare, with her hair standing on end, and her eyes wild and red with weeping. She rushed past me into the drawing-room, screaming, 'Mummy, Mummy, Mummy!' and, flinging herself into her mother's arms, burst into floods of tears.

I wasn't going to miss a scene like this, so I took up a strategic position behind the half-open door, and waited, while Clare was gradually calmed by her mother into a state fit for speech.

'What is it, darling?' she said, when the sobs had been choked back into isolated hiccoughs. 'Tell me what it's all about.'

'Oh, Mummy, it's Alec. They've taken him to a Nursing Home. Mummy, he's got to have an operation – tonight!'

'An operation?' said her father. 'What d'you mean? What for?'

'He suddenly had the most awful sort of attack after lunch, and I thought he was going to die, and then the doctor came, and they took him away – oh, it was awful – in an ambulance! They wouldn't let me go in it. He looked all peculiar, he –' she burst into tears again, burying her head in her mother's lap, from the smothered sound of the sobs that I heard.

'Yes, but for heaven's sake, Clare, what *for*?'

'Appendicitis!' came a muffled wail.

Her father, who had been holding his breath in his agitation, let it all out on a sigh of relief. 'Is that all? Why, that's nothing these days, darling.'

'Nothing, you call it? I think it's g-ghastly. Oh, poor Alec! Oh, Mummy, suppose something goes wrong, he's never been ill before, what if he can't take gas properly or something? Oh –'

'Now, Clare, darling, don't be hysterical. People have their appendixes out every day of the week. It's sure to be all right; especially as they've caught it at once.' Her mother was being wonderfully calm, as she undoubtedly always would be in any crisis. 'When are they going to operate?'

'Six o'clock. Can we go there, d'you suppose?'

'Yes, of course. Where is he? Wimpole Street? We'll go along at once.'

'Who's doing the operation?' asked Mr Vaughan.

'Some butcher called Wilson-Stokes. Have you ever heard of him?'

'Old Stokey? I should think I had. Why, we were at Cambridge together. Grand lad, Stokey, he'll look after Alec all right, don't you worry. Most amusing devil; I remember he and I once had a terrific row about a girl in a draper's shop. She – '

'John, dear, stop reminiscing, and go and ring up a taxi. And get Clare some brandy, that's what she needs.'

I had been so engrossed in this human drama, that it was not until I skipped out of the way before Mr Vaughan should come out, that my nose told me what to expect in the kitchen. At first sight, I thought the whole stove was on fire, but then I saw that it was only my crumpets blazing merrily away under the grill. I dashed water on to them, to quench the flames, and went out to the dustbin to throw away the blackened remains before anyone could see what I had done. I couldn't think what the faint roaring noise was, and it was not until the kitchen began to smell like an air-raid that I realized that I had forgotten to turn off the taps, after putting out the flames.

I opened the window wide, but Mrs Vaughan came in, and nearly fainted as the atmosphere hit her.

'Goodness, Monica, what have you been doing?'

'Cooking crumpets, madam.'

'Well, they smell rather funny. Never mind, we shan't be wanting any tea anyway; we all have to go out. Poor Mr Chesterton has to have an operation for appendicitis, isn't that bad luck?'

'Well, I am sorry to hear that. Who'd have thought it?' I said, feigning great surprise at the news; 'I hope everything'll go off all right, madam, I'm sure.'

'Oh, yes, of course, we don't expect any trouble. I thought it would be a good thing for Mrs Chesterton to stay here for a bit, though, it's so much nearer the Home. Would you make up the bed in the little spare room before you go? – and lay supper for three – I don't know when we'll be back. Then tomorrow Miss Clare is going to fetch little Peter and his nurse over; they can go into the big spare room, if they bring his cot. It'll be nice to have the little boy here – won't it? – ' She gazed at me anxiously, as my jaw was dropping a bit at the thought of all the extra work. She was afraid I was going to say: 'I've only got one pair of hands', or, 'It's not my work,' so I pulled myself together, and struggled to appear the old family servant, the rock – equal to any crisis.

'I'll try and get Maud to stay on for the whole day,' she went on, 'then we ought to be able to manage all right.' Wails of, 'Mummy, *do* let's go!' came from the hall, so she hurried off, throwing a few injunctions, such as 'Cold beef,' and 'Hot bottle,' at me over her shoulder.

When 'in service' one has a rather cold-blooded

tendency to regard the emotions and hazards of one's employers' lives with a certain detachment – almost as if they were people in a play, and the kitchen was the back row of the pit. I was surprised, therefore, to find that the thought of the nice blond Alec Chesterton being slit open at six o'clock quite worried me.

When I arrived at the flat next morning, I didn't have to wait till I called Mrs Vaughan, to hear the news. The sight of the dining-room reassured me. They would not have made such a hearty meal, and washed it down with a bottle of champagne, if all had not gone well. I was able to greet Mrs Vaughan with a bright and appropriate smile, when she woke, as usual, as I put down the tea-tray.

'I'm so glad the operation went off all right, madam,' I said.

'Yes, isn't it splendid? But however did you know?'

'I just *knew*, madam,' I said mysteriously, 'I have a *feeling* about things sometimes.' I gave her a penetrating look, charged with psychic meaning, and went out, leaving her sitting bolt upright, staring after me in great astonishment.

I had been told not to wake Clare, and she slept on until long after Maud had arrived. She was fascinated by the whole story, and pressed me for medical details of the operation, which I was unable to supply, though I made a few up to keep her going. When Clare woke up, and yelled for her breakfast (none of this family ever rang bells – they had got so used to them not being answered), Maud insisted on taking in her tray. She was in there quite a quarter of an hour, and came out bursting with information. She was retailing it to me, when Mrs Vaughan came in, to ask her if she would be able to put in more time at the flat.

Maud sucked her teeth. 'I'd be very pleased to, 'm, I'm sure, but I'll have to ask Mum. She gets a funny head, you know, and doesn't like to be left. I think it'll be O.K. though, as a matter of fact, because my sister Ivy's at home for a bit now. She's theatrical, you know, resting before the Panto season. Principal Boy at Nottingham – *Babes in the Wood*, it is, 'm.' I had heard a lot about this Ivy, famed in the Theatre Royal or Hippodrome of many a provincial town as 'Gloria May, the Sweetheart of Bradford' (or Huddersfield, or Kidderminster, as the case might be).

'Shall I pop over at lunch-time, 'm, and see what Mum says?'

'Thank you so much, Maud. I do hope it'll be all right. It would be such a help to have you.'

Clare went off later on to fetch her nurse and child, and Maud and I put in some good work, making the spare rooms a home from home. We had the same ideas about house-work, both favouring the dust-under-the-bed method, our motto being: 'What the eye don't see, etc.' We got on very well together, especially when Mrs Vaughan was not hovering round us, making suggestions, and giving us the moral support of her conversation.

Maud 'popped' just before one, and soon afterwards the Chesterton *ménage* arrived, complete with all the etceteras that make a small child as bulky to travel with as an American heiress. I went down to help unload the car, and Mrs Vaughan and I had quite a tussle with a spring mattress, until we discovered that it came out quite easily if one pushed and the other pulled, instead of both tugging from opposite sides.

Peter sat up in a high chair at lunch, and pulled my apron strings undone every time I passed his corner of the table. He kept it dark from his nurse, for whom he seemed to have no very great affection. I didn't know her as well as he did, but from the look of her I didn't blame him. I should have thought the sight of her horse-face alone would have been enough to give any child inhibitions, apart from the fact that she exuded a most unpleasant smell of mothballs. She didn't seem to take much to me, either, and I wondered if we were fated to be mortal enemies. Sure enough, it was written by the hand of fate in my teacup that very afternoon.

Mrs Vaughan and her daughter went back to the Nursing Home soon after lunch, and the horse went for a trot with the pram. Maud arrived while I was washing up, with the glad news that her mother had given her consent, and, furthermore, as Aunt Maggie was coming to keep her company that afternoon, Gloria May had promised to shed the radiance of her presence on us, by coming to tea in the kitchen. I was thrilled at the idea of seeing a Principal Boy without tights and ostrich feathers; I had never met one off-stage, and Maud could hardly wait for me to meet her. She was terrifically proud of this sister, whom she regarded as a being from quite another world, as far removed from us in station as our employers.

Nurse was back by the time Gloria arrived, and she popped out of her room to see what she was like. She sniffed at what she saw, and went disdainfully back to her stable. I think she was jealous of Ivy's teeth, which had rushed to the front of her mouth in an even more dazzling profusion than hers.

The fame and adoration of the Provinces had not turned Ivy's head at all. She was just a very colourful edition of Maud, with the same jolly simplicity of heart. Her hair was curled in many sausages of brassy-gold, and jingling bracelets stretched from wrist to elbow over her dress of brightest emerald green – but then, you've got to have a bit of style if you're on the stage. She made a good tea.

'It's a good thing Mr Mosei likes a few curves in the right places,' she remarked, accepting a second slice of cake. 'Wouldn't suit me to have to watch my diet, I can tell you. Anyway, who wants to be skin and bone? Look at Sylvia Farrar, forty if she's a day, and looks fifty without her make-up.'

'Who's she?' asked Maud, hanging on her words, with rapt adoration.

'Principal Girl in *The Babes*. Lord, what a cat, and sour! My dear, don't speak of it. There'll be plenty of fights between her and Yours Truly before this season's over, or my name's not Gloria May.'

When we had finished tea, Maud said, 'Shall we tell the cups, Ive?'

'Not me,' said her sister, with a superstitious shudder. 'You don't catch me telling my fortune before the first night. Worst thing out for luck. You do yours though, go on.'

Maud peered into my cup, breathing heavily. 'Can't make head nor tail of this, dear. I believe this is a common quality tea. Ooh, whatever's this, though? A snake, look! Enemies and treachery. That's not a bit nice. Have another go, I should. Fill your cup up again, dear.'

'No, this is all right,' I said, 'I'd call this a horse at the bottom, wouldn't you, Maud?'

'I would, and kicking too.'

I was quite moved by this unmistakable sign from the beyond. It gave me a good excuse not to waste energy being friendly to Nurse, if fate had willed it otherwise.

Maud made a wish on hers, and there was quite a nice little crescent moon in her cup. 'Ooh, I say!' she breathed. 'Romance!'

'What did you wish about, Maud?'

'Ah, that's tellin'. Ask me no questions, I tell no lies.'

'Come off it, ducks,' said Gloria May, convulsed with toothy laughter. 'If you want to keep anything dark, you shouldn't let Mum know. She told me all about the postman looking sideways at you in Edgware Road. Lord! That reminds me, I promised I'd get home before Aunt Maggie goes; I must be toddling along.' She got up, drawing her fur-collared coat round her. 'Good-bye, all! It's been ever so nice to have met you, Miss Dixon.' She went off, with a flash of teeth, and a jingling wave of the hand, leaving us feeling very flat and dissatisfied with a life which made it possible for Nurse to summon one to the dining-room, by ringing the bell for more milk. I took it in with a glower of simmering hatred, quite worthy of the Demon King himself, in one of Ivy's pantomimes.

According to the voluble bulletins that Mrs Vaughan gave us every morning, while ordering the meals, Clare's husband was continuing to make good progress, and no anxiety was felt about him. There was no reason, therefore, why a dinner party, which had been brewing for some time, should not be held.

'Are you sure you and Maud can manage all right by

yourselves?' Mrs Vaughan asked me. 'We shall be ten, I think, but I can easily get someone in to help with the waiting.'

I said, 'No, no,' proudly, and assured her that it would be a mere nothing to us. I didn't want to miss the amusing part, which was the handing round, and listening to scraps of conversation; also, we two fell over each other enough, as it was, without having another body to add to the confusion.

Confusion is the right word for the state we were in on the evening of the party. In contrast to the first dinner I had cooked at the Vaughans', this time, everything was going wrong.

It started by my dropping a milk bottle on the floor, leaving myself with nothing to make a White Sauce for the cauliflower.

'I'll pop out for some,' said Maud amiably, but by the time she got back, I had discovered that, though there would be White Sauce, there was no cauliflower to put in it.

'That greengrocer hasn't sent one,' said Maud, 'I know his sort, I'll give him What For.' She was just going to pop again, when Clare came shouting that they wanted tea for three in the drawing-room, with Anchovy toast and Plum Cake. (How typical of Miss Nitchin to be here again today.) Would we also mind hurrying-up with the nursery tea, as Peter was screaming with hunger.

Maud had to stay and help get the teas, as I was too busy cooking to be able to do more than watch the toast. I rang up the greengrocer as soon as I had a spare moment, and reviled him.

'Haven't got a boy in the shop,' he said, unabashed. 'Nor shall have before six, if then.'

'Maud, you'll have to go, we want potatoes, and onions, too.'

'O.K., dear, just wait till I take in this tea. What a to-do, eh?' She went out again, into the rain, and while she was gone, one or two bells kept me rushing about; once for more hot water, once for more jam sandwiches (Nurse), and once to open the door to a man selling tickets for the Fireman's Ball. All this meant that my Jugged Hare, which ought to have been put into the oven long ago, was making no progress at all. I couldn't find half the things to put in it, either.

'Maud, Maud!' when she came back laden with vegetables, and dripping rain-water on to the floor. 'Where's that Cooking Port we had left over from last week?' We started a frenzied searching.

'Can't see for looking,' said Maud, standing on a chair to look on the top shelf of the cupboard. 'Oh, my Gordon!' she cried, losing her balance, and staggering to the ground. 'Don't you remember, dear? We drank it that evening when I had the blues and you had the colly-wobbles.'

This was ghastly. I saw myself having to jug the hare with water and cochineal, and leaving the rest to the imagination of the diners. There was only one thing to do.

'We'll have to get a bottle out of the wine cupboard. The key's in the hall table. Maud, you do it, quick, while they're at tea.'

'Not me, I daren't. You go, dear.'

'No, you.'

We tossed for it in the end, and Maud lost.

'I'll take the cheapest-looking,' she whispered, tiptoeing into the hall with heavy thuds. Needless to say, Nurse chose this moment to finish her tea, and come out of the dining-room.

'Tra-la-la!' sang Maud with artificial unconcern, pretending to be sorting letters on the table, until Nurse and Peter had passed into the drawing-room.

'Here,' said Maud, rushing back a minute later, and waving a bottle triumphantly, 'this is Port, isn't it?'

After a lot of hacking and delving, she got the cork out, and it was not till then that I took a closer look at the bottle, and saw the film of dust and age that clothed it, and the tell-tale bits of crusted black seal still clinging to the neck.

'I took one of the shabbiest I could find,' said Maud cheerfully. 'Phew! You should have heard my heart beat. Haven't had such a bit of excitement since father died.'

Quite exciting for the hare, too, to be jugged in rare old Vintage Port. I used it liberally, and poured the rest into a jug, so that I could bury the evidence of that bottle deep in the dustbin.

We washed up the tea, so as to get it out of the way, and I shook a careless soapy hand in the air, and deposited a few suds in the soup. It didn't seem to make any difference to the taste, and, 'What the eye don't see –' said Maud.

She laid the table, and then came back to help me with the last stages of cooking. You wouldn't have thought two people in one room could possibly get in one another's way so much, or make quite such a commotion and mess. Even Mrs Vaughan who, having at last got rid of the Nitchin by offering to pay her taxi, came in to see how things were going, retreated before the clamour of battle. There simply was no room for her; Maud and I had developed into about twenty people, with outsize feet.

Maud had already put on her clean party apron, as it was now nearly half past seven, and the guests were due at a quarter to eight. I was going to change in the last minute, so as to be sure of not dirtying mine, and I was justified in this precaution, when a piercing howl from her, as she opened a tin of cherries to decorate the pudding, brought Clare out into the hall in a pair of cami-knickers.

'Fruit juice!' wailed Maud. 'All over my apron, and I haven't got another!'

'Soak it in salt water, quick!' cried Clare, running about looking like a picture on a magazine cover. 'Gosh, the bell! Let me get back to my room before you open the door.' She fled. I couldn't answer the bell, shiny mess as I was from cooking and turmoil, and it had rung again, before I had found Maud an old, but fairly clean apron of mine in the dresser drawer.

'You're too early,' said Clare, coming out into the hall again, as a loud guffaw announced that it was only Frances and husband. She took them into the drawing-room, doing up her dress as she went.

The other guests were not so punctual. This, I believe, is a source of annoyance to the good cook, who has everything ready on time, but it is always a blessing to such as me.

I cleaned myself up a bit while they were having cock-tails, and carried in the soup, while Maud announced dinner. We had arranged that we would each do one side of the table, and this worked quite well, except that there was one rather pathetic man at the end who didn't seem to belong to either of us, and was constantly being forgotten. I don't believe he got half the things handed to him, but perhaps it was as well, for he looked the dyspeptic sort.

Clare made Maud's face shine red with embarrassment

through the thick white coat of powder that she had applied for the occasion by saying loudly, as she handed the soup: 'Oh, you got a clean apron, Maudie, dear, you do look smart!'

The hare had a success worthy of the extravagance of its ingredients. 'What *a delicious* dish!' said a large purple velvet woman on Mr Vaughan's right, 'I really must be greedy and have another helping.'

'I hope it doesn't put you under the table, that's all,' I thought, holding the dish while she spooned out a lot of the Fine Old Fruity gravy.

Serving the dinner between the two of us was quite a hectic business and we should have been even more flustered if it had not been such an informal affair. Mr Vaughan helped by stumbling about with the drinks, and his wife popped up and down in her usual style, getting bread, and thinking she heard the telephone ring. A brief lull in the babel of conversation was filled by a penetrating whisper from Maud, as she handed Frances the sweet course: 'Come on, Miss, tickle out the cherries! We haven't got all night.'

In spite of the many set-backs that had occurred during its preparation, the dinner seemed to go down all right, helped along by the lavishness of the host in the matter of alcohol. The men were so obviously dug in for a long session with the port and brandy, that Maud and I abandoned all hope of clearing the table for some time, and sat down to stuff ourselves with leavings among the piles of dirty crockery that littered the kitchen. The best part of any party is always the discussion and criticism of the guests that one indulges in afterwards, whether one has participated in a below- or an above-stairs capacity. Maud was quite vindictive for her. She had taken exception to a nut-crackery woman in a violent shade of cyclamen.

'I never did like that Mrs Holden, and I never shall,' she declared. 'I take people as they come and she comes very unpleasant. Messing about with the sweet, she was, as if it was mud pies, and then didn't take but only a spoonful. "Well!" I felt like saying: "If you don't want to buy the watch, don't breathe on the works."'

'She drank enough, anyway. I saw her fairly lapping it up.'

'That's right. Would you believe it, she had some of that cream stuff – demented cream, or whatever they call it, and then didn't say no to a glass of brandy.'

An uproar of male voices indicated that the gents were joining the ladies, and a higher, more piercing wail indicated that the noise had woken Peter.

Maud and I cleared away the rest of the things in the dining-room, and were continuing our gossip over the washing up, when Nurse came padding into the kitchen – a most unappetizing figure in black carpet slippers and a green flannel dressing-gown. Her streaky hair, smelling more strongly of moth-balls than ever, hung down her back like so much seaweed.

'They've woken my little boy,' she said, 'I never heard of such a thing.' She turned her schoolmistress eye on us as if we were to blame. 'I'm going to see if a little warm milk won't send him off.'

'Oh, Nurse, I'm ever so sorry,' I said, 'there isn't a drop in the place till the milkman comes tomorrow.'

She had never heard of such a thing as this either. She took it as a sign of personal spite. 'I shall have to speak to Mrs Vaughan in the morning,' she said. 'I shall have to make it clear to her that I'm not at *all* accustomed to this sort of thing. I've never had to do with it before, and I don't wish to start now.' She was gone, with an indignant whisk of the seaweed. I was too tired to do more than giggle feebly, and Maud was seriously shocked at such an exhibition of superiority from one whom she didn't consider Real Class. Peter evidently soon decided that it was better to be asleep than to have to contemplate his nurse, for the wails ceased before long.

Mrs Vaughan came into the kitchen to say how well it had all gone off. I thought for the thousandth time what a mercy it is that mistresses don't see the back-stage details of a dinner-party, they probably wouldn't eat a thing if they did.

We didn't finish till well after eleven o'clock, but the

next day was a Sunday, which meant that I didn't have to arrive quite so early in the morning.

I saw Nurse buttonhole Mrs Vaughan after breakfast, and tell her some long story, with much nodding of the head and raising of the eyebrows. I thought it was probably about me, so I was not surprised when I was summoned after Nurse had gone.

'I don't quite know what it's all about,' said my mistress, smiling, 'but Nurse seems annoyed about something. You must be careful not to upset her. It may be only a little misunderstanding, but I do like harmony in my household.' I was going to stick up for myself, but she, who hated having to 'speak to' anyone, hastily picked up the telephone and dialled a number, to prevent any further discussion of the subject.

I slouched out of the room, muttering gloomily, and met Peter in the hall, dressed to go out. He was amusing himself while he waited for his nurse, by methodically straightening out each separate fringe of a Persian rug. I stopped to have a word with him – here was someone, at least, who didn't annoy me. As far as he was concerned, my sole use in the world was to provide food, so he promptly seized me by the hand, and led me to his favourite biscuit tin in the kitchen. The child was ambidextrous, so it always had to be two of everything, so that he could have one in each hand. He was sitting on the table, taking bites out of each biscuit in turn, when a camphorated tornado blew in through the door, swooped down on him, and bore him off, screaming, and dribbling tears and biscuit crumbs all the way to the front door.

'Now I've told you time again, you're not to keep running into the kitchen. If you want a biscuit, you can ask Nanny for it, the kitchen is not the place for little boys.'

The door slammed on this remark, and I was left seething. I suppose she thought the child would pick up vices or something if he spent too long in my company. I was longing for Maud to arrive, so that I could unload my grievances on to her good-natured ear. Surely she was very late? I looked at the clock and saw that she was nearly an hour after her time. I was thinking that pretty soon I would be able to put off no longer the various unpleasant jobs that I had been leaving for her to do, when the back bell rang, and I opened the door to an extremely dirty small boy in trousers cut down from a full-grown man's, bunched round his waist with a bit of string. He handed me an envelope which said, 'Mrs Vaughan, by hand,' so, telling him to wait, I took it along to the drawing-room. Mrs Vaughan read it, tut-tutted in a distressed way, and handed it to me.

Dear Madam (I read),
I am sorry to say that Mum has taken a Coma. She lays still as she has done since 5 this morning and Dr Bright says not to leave her. Hope you can spare me Madam.

Will let you know when I can come back. Please tell Monica Mr V. must have clean towels today.

With apologies, Madam, yours truly,

M. BUXTON (Maud)

This was most upsetting, especially the touching evidence of Maud's devotion to duty. Mrs Vaughan asked me to get her the medical dictionary, while she scribbled a note in reply, so that she could look up all about Diabetic comas.

The small boy was still standing where I had left him, but on one leg now, with the other twisted round it in an uncomfortable-looking way. I gave him the note, and sixpence from Mrs Vaughan, and impressed on him that he was to go straight back to Maud.

When she was worried about anything, Mrs Vaughan always had to vent her anxiety in a flow of words, so I had to go along to the drawing-room and lend an ear. She didn't really want answers, as she was quite happy to conduct a conversation with herself; but she liked to have someone in the room, for company's sake.

I got on with polishing the fire-dogs while she talked.

'Very worrying,' she was saying. 'Poor Maud, I do feel so sorry for her. Of course, her mother's been ill for a long time, but this does seem to be a turn for the worse. A coma – rather serious, I'm afraid, but on the other hand it may be nothing much – perhaps the doctor's a scaremonger. I hope they'll take her to hospital … Oh, of course, they will, they always do if it's serious. Unless, of course, she can't be moved. She'd be better in hospital, though. I wonder if I could do any good by going round there? I think I will, if she isn't better tomorrow. One might be a nuisance, though, I wouldn't want Maud to think I was interfering. I wonder when she'll come back – she won't stay away long unless her mother's really bad, then we should have to get someone in to help you. I think I'll leave it for the moment, until we hear from Maud. You must just skimp the work, we shan't mind. I'll help you where I can. D'you think you can manage? I don't want to ask too much of you.'

'Yes, madam,' I said, making my first and last contribution to the conversation. I had finished my polishing, and Mrs Vaughan seemed to have temporarily dried up, so I left her, as I had a thousand things to do.

I didn't know where to start. There were so many things that Maud usually did, such as beds, baths, and boots, as well as my own share of the housework, and all the cooking. We had drifted into a sort of slap-dash routine, and, between us, had got through the work fairly easily, but my brain reeled at the thought of doing it all by myself. However, Mrs Vaughan had said 'skimp the work', so I took her at her word, and it was an understatement for the shirking I indulged in that morning.

I made beds by the simple, if unhygienic, method of

pulling up the clothes without untucking them, and barely stayed long enough in the bathroom to put the tooth-brushes in the mugs and fold up the bath-mat. I closed my eyes to the three layers of dirt round the bath, indicating where Nurse, Peter, and Clare had rid themselves of some of the grime of London. The next person in would be Mr Vaughan, who was short-sighted, and would only add a fresh level anyway. Nevertheless, there was still enough that had to be done to keep me panting about the place, trying to dust, sweep, and cook lunch for four people and a baby all at the same time.

I wished it had not been the day for Peter to have brains; I always had to nerve myself for the ordeal of handling them, and this morning my resistance was weak. I thought of Maud's mother in her coma and wished it was me. There is no doubt that drudgery is embittering to the soul, and the sympathy that I should have been feeling for the Buxton family was replaced by a rather sour resentment.

'Poor Maud and all that,' I thought, starting to wash up the breakfast things, when I could stand the sight of the egg- and marmalade-encrusted plates no longer, 'but if ever there was a case of "One pair of hands", it's now.'

It was a horrible lunch I gave them. Stringy, sodden cabbage, overdone beef, and lumpy custard were among the things that made it memorable. Laying the table in a hurry, I had forgotten various things, and I had to keep running to the kitchen for them, in between handing round. I had also forgotten to make any coffee, and as they were going to a concert they had no time to wait while I made some.

Almost the worst part of the whole thing was the confounded tolerance of the Vaughan family. They didn't mind a bit, and kept making allowances for me, which was more annoying than if they had reviled me, as it put me in the wrong for feeling ill-used. However, there was always Nurse to pin a bit of spare rage on to; she was quite willing to add to the gaiety of life by demanding extras, such as a Swiss roll for Peter's tea. I made no objection as I was beginning to feel resigned, in a sort of stark Russian way, and one thing more to do couldn't possibly make me feel any worse. Today was Sunday anyway, and I was supposed to go off at six o'clock, which I determined to do, whether I had finished my work or not. It amused me to think that there had been a time, far back at the start of my kitchen career, when I should have had no peace of mind or sleep if I had gone home leaving any jobs undone. Domestic service had had a most demoralizing effect on me. It was a very different person from that conscientious enthusiast of over a year ago who now banged the door behind her on empty coal-scuttles, a supper laid with only the bare necessities, tea-things in the sink, and three pieces of a broken plate lying in the middle of the dirty kitchen floor.

Chapter Fifteen

Looking back on my last few weeks at the Vaughans' I can never make out why I didn't throw up the sponge sooner than I did. Maud's mother continued to 'lay like a log, madam', and this and other circumstances combined to result in my carrying on by myself. Mrs Vaughan and I had a heart-to-heart talk a few days after we heard that Maud was not yet coming back.

I was laying the fire in the drawing-room, a task that was supposed to be done before breakfast but never was. My mistress never said anything about it, and didn't seem to mind my crashing about in the hearth while she was writing letters and telephoning to tradesmen.

'Well, Monica,' she said, raising her voice so as to be heard above the clatter of me raking out cinders, 'I really don't know what to say. I've made inquiries, but it seems impossible to find a char who's half-way nice. I'd rather the flat went dirty than have to put up with some of the drunken old cripples they've offered me. – Yes, what is it, dear?' as her husband poked his head round the door. He didn't see me as the sofa was between him and my kneeling form, so he spoke without reticence.

'Where the hell has that imbecile hidden my nail-scissors? I wish you'd speak to her, dearest. Of all the half-witted sluts we've ever had …'

'*Ruhig! Ist im Zimmer!*' hissed his wife, whose German education was better than her French.

'*Mein Gott,* is she? *Je n'ai pas vu,*' he mumbled, withdrawing his head hurriedly. Mrs Vaughan was so upset to think that I might have been offended that, to show I didn't mind, I had to fall in with the suggestion she now put to me.

'I was wondering,' she said, 'whether, if I gave you a bit extra, you could possibly carry on by yourself for the time being. You seem to be managing quite well – providing you're not getting too tired? It seems hardly worth trying to find a non-existent char when we don't know when Maud may come back. What d'you think? I don't want to slave-drive you. You mustn't mind Mr Vaughan,' she added, laughing uncertainly, 'you know what men are – always saying things they don't mean. I do hope it didn't upset you?' She looked so concerned that I had to say: 'I'm sure I can manage myself, madam,' in order to show her there was no ill-feeling.

She said that she would give me thirty-five shillings a week, and added the extra bait that Clare would not be staying much longer as she was taking her husband away to convalesce. Nurse was staying on, needless to say, but I was getting so used to loathing her that I should almost have missed her if she had gone.

I was in a rut altogether. Exhaustion gradually began to induce in my brain a coma quite worthy of Mrs Buxton, although my body was not recumbent like hers, but walked about in grim and automatic toil. I don't blame my mistress, for I had brought it on myself, and she really had no idea how tired I was. She merely thought me rather more than abnormally stupid and spent her time making allowances for each fresh nonsense that I made, which encouraged me to make still more to see how much she would stand.

Sometimes, in order to cheer myself up, I tried dressing-up and going out in the evening, but it was not a success. I had lost the Party Spirit – it had gone down the plug-hole of the sink, or been thrown into the dustbin and buried under tin cans and cabbage stalks.

On days when my employers were going out to dinner they generally let me go home at about seven, which gave me the opportunity to attempt a little weary whoopee. I arrived home on one of these evenings to find an invitation to go to the theatre and dance afterwards. I decided to go, although I didn't know the people very well, and I had never felt less like gaiety in my life.

I quite enjoyed the theatre because it gave me the chance of having a nice little nap. I woke up in the intervals and said: 'Marvellous! I do think it's good, don't you?' so nobody noticed that I had no idea whether the play was musical comedy or a Russian tragedy.

A good supper revived me: it was lovely to eat food that I hadn't cooked myself, and I had quite a light-hearted dance or two, untroubled by housemaid's knee.

'Thank Heaven for alcohol!' I kept thinking, amazed at the way in which those feet, which had been trailing around all day behind brooms and carpet-sweepers, were doing the rumba. My knell was sounded, however, by the voice that said, 'There will be an interval for the glasses to be cleared from the tables!'

Pretty soon after that I began to wilt, and it was unfortunate that I had to do it while dancing with a hot-blooded gentleman of South American extraction. I suddenly felt like death and drooped on his shoulder, hooking myself on with my chin to save myself from falling like a log. He thought this was the Invitation to the Waltz and got very Trans-Atlantic. His passionate grip had the advantage of supporting me and keeping me on my feet, so I could just bear it until the end of the dance released me from his greasy clutches. I staggered to a chair and said: 'I really ought to go home. I'm rather tired, I've been working so hard all day.' No one knew what at, they were the sort of people who would have raised their eyebrows and laughed uncomfortably if they had known they were entertaining a cook-general.

'I weel take you 'ome,' said Black Pedro instantly, and I had to choose between this very repulsive prospect and going on to a night club with the others. A good look at Pedro decided me. We all got into taxis and I found myself walking as though in my sleep into a dim and airless haunt of gaiety six times as sordid as any basement that ever smelt of greens.

I sat down at a corner table with the rest, and soon they all got up to dance. Pedro asked me and I shook my head, which suddenly weighed ten stone so that I had to put my arms on to the table and drop it on to them.

The band was playing 'Boom, boom, zinca boom, zinca boom!' or was it in my head? No, because there was a bee there, singing … singing, to the boom, zinca boom … Ees the matter? said Pedro from the other side of London. Boom said the bee, said the boom, said the … you eell? I am swimming in waves of rhythm … I am sinking … boom, zinca boom, sinking boom, sinking …

My heart woke me by dropping out of my breast with a crash. I was instantly conscious of a strong and unfamiliar smell, and raising my head slightly, I saw with surprise that a fat white hand with crimson nails was attached to one of my elbows like a growth.

'I've brought you some aspirin, dear, make you feel better. Just the ticket when you've passed out,' said a hoarse voice in my ear. I was bolt upright now and fully conscious of where I was.

Pedro had disappeared, and the others, I suppose, were still dancing somewhere on the dim and faraway sea of the dance floor. I was alone at the table except for a raddled but motherly creature, who had for the moment abandoned her duties of 'hostess' to minister to what she thought was a Dead Drunk.

My one thought was to escape, I couldn't even thank her. I pushed her away and, leaping to my feet, made for the door, followed by the delighted sniggers of the band, who had evidently been watching the whole comedy of my disgrace.

This episode, with the consequent necessity for apologies to my hostess, whom I have never seen since, and the death-like Hangover that enveloped me all the next day, discouraged me from much more sociability. I had to attend an occasional dinner party, and there were one or two rather pathetic incidents, such as the time when I went fast asleep with my head pillowed on the shoulder of a High Court judge, and once when I lost all chance of success with a French Count who discovered, when he kissed my hand, that it smelt strongly of that well-known perfume, 'Bouquet des Oignons'.

I had got into the state of thinking that life was bounded by gas-stoves and grease, and saw no reason to imagine that it could ever hold anything more for me. This melancholy thought made me sour and disagreeable during the few hours I spent at home, and by no means a ray of sunshine at the Vaughans'. My sulky apathy was beginning to tell on even my mistress's nerves, though she never ticked me off. I noticed her once or twice checking an impatient exclamation at my incompetence, but she was far too kind ever to suggest 'making a change', however trying I was, quite apart from the fact that she knew that the species 'Cook-General' was comparatively rare. The poor woman's flat was in a terrible state. The smuts and dust of London, which always get the upper hand unless resisted with methodical zeal, had consolidated their position, undeterred by my feeble opposition with dirty dusters and brushes clogged with fluff.

Once when Mr Vaughan had his glasses on he caught sight of his tarnished golf cups, and he also discovered that the mustard and pepper pots had reverted to their former condition of emptiness. I was just on my way in with the joint and two veg., but I waited outside the door until he had finished saying: 'Really, dearest, why don't you speak to her? You put up with anything; it's thoroughly bad for a lazy girl like that.'

There was a pause, presumably for Mrs Vaughan to tap her head significantly, and I heard her murmur something about 'Poor thing … can't help it'.

The first of December is a date that is engraved on my memory, for it was the day on which I woke at last to the realization of a New Dawn. I can't understand why it didn't happen before; I can only suppose that it was this sort of trance of fatigue that I was in that made me accept my dreary lot for so long. It was certainly not curiosity any longer or interest in seeing Life in the Raw. I had found out all I wanted to know about kitchen affairs, and a great deal too much about the squalor attached thereto.

It was while I was washing up after lunch, always one of the lowest spots of the day, that I suddenly saw the light.

Something seemed to click in my brain. The curtain of fog went up with a rush, and it became all at once crystal clear and filled with the dazzling white light of reason.

'This is no sort of life for a girl!' The words rang in my head like a bugle call. The back-door bell rang, too, and the baker was quite startled by the joyous reception I gave him. I almost embraced him in my new-found lightness of heart. It didn't matter that he was one of the most drooping and depressed-looking creatures who ever walked this earth; I bubbled at him, hardly knowing what I was saying.

'I'm going! I'm leaving! For ever, I mean. A new day has dawned. I can't stand it any longer. Oh, baker, baker, congratulate me, I'm so happy!'

I seized him by the hand, and he suffered it to be pumped up and down, saying gloomily 'What a song and dance about getting the sack, I must say.'

'Sack? What are you talking about? I've fired myself

this time. I'm walking on air, I tell you. I'm going to Live, Laugh, and Love! Can you waltz?'

'I did used to in me younger days ...' he said hesitatingly, but with a sparkle of something almost like wistful gaiety beginning to gleam in his eye.

To the strains of the 'Blue Danube', panting and gasping as we whirled and bumped, we were rounding the table for the third time when our progress was impeded by a solid body which had stepped in through the door just in time to make a collision inevitable.

'Monica!' said Nurse in a choking, scandalized voice as she picked herself up out of the coal-bucket, '*Get* on with your work, and don't make yourself cheap with the tradesmen.'

She had got so used to my pretending to her to be more or less deaf and dumb, as I had for the last week or two so as to save myself the trouble of talking to her, that she was quite startled by the spate of words that now escaped me. She retreated before them into the hall, protesting feebly, and fending me off with upraised hands. She backed straight into the drawing-room, and I heard her say: 'I'm afraid Monica has gone out of her mind. Shall I dial 999?'

I pushed the baker out of the back door, and just had time to seize a carrot and be discovered chopping it with sane and meticulous accuracy when Mrs Vaughan came running in.

'Nurse said –' she began, and then stopped and looked at me wonderingly. '*Is* anything the matter, Monica? You look quite flushed.'

'I don't feel quite the thing, 'm,' I mumbled. 'Vertigo. Mother says I ought to take a rest – go away or something. "Monica," she said to me last night, "You're over-taxing your strength. You'll kill yourself if you go on like this." I never was strong from a child, you know, madam.'

Illness had got me out of the Chilford House job without acrimony, so I thought I had better fall back on it again this time.

I rather wished I hadn't, for Mrs Vaughan, though secretly rejoicing at the opportunity to get rid of me without hurting my feelings, was terribly concerned about my health. She insisted on feeling the back of my neck, which she declared was stinging hot and showed I had a temperature. I managed to convince her that I could hold together until she found someone to replace me. I tried to strike a note of wilting but courageous suffering, which was difficult when the only thing wrong with me was a fever of delirious joy.

Distressed, she went away to ring up all the agencies she knew, and I, feeling rather a cad, decided to prepare a very special dinner to salve my conscience.

Mrs Vaughan went out to follow up one or two likely trails, throwing parting injunctions at me 'not to overdo it' and to ' take two aspirins in a glass of hot milk'.

She didn't get back till after six, by which time an exotic chicken dish was simmering itself to a rich perfection in the oven. She found me in the drawing-room, whither I had gone in response to a roar from Mr Vaughan: 'Curse this infernal machine! Monica! Come and get this damned number for me before I –'

The whole trouble was that the poor darling's fingers were too fat and stubby to fit into the holes of the dial. He had tried yelling: 'Operator, operator!' into the mouth-piece, and been maddened by the penetrating and impersonal 'burr-r-r-r' that mocked him in answer. By the time I came to his rescue he had forgotten what number he was trying to get. When he eventually found it, after much hunting through a jumble of papers in his pocket-book, I decided not to dial it, but to dial 'O' and let him ask them for it. I thought it would be good for 'O's' patronizing smugness to listen to a sample of his extensive vocabulary.

His wife came in when he was in the middle of it, so with a final shout of 'I shall write to *The Times*!' he gave it up and decided to write a postcard instead.

I left them as I thought she might want to tell him about me, for women will never learn that if there is one subject that bores a man more than any other it is the servant problem in his own house.

She came into the kitchen quite soon and said: 'Well,

you'll be pleased to hear that we're going out to dinner; you can go home when you like. That'll be nice, won't it?'

I could have cried, had it not been for the spring of happiness that was still bubbling inside me. 'The chicken, madam!' I cried, agonized. 'A special dish. And the *zabaglione*!'

'Oh dear, I didn't think you would have started yet. I had said roasted, hadn't I? We can't very well get out of going to the Welds' now, I asked them if they'd have us. Wouldn't it keep till tomorrow? We could have it heated up … Oh, by the way, talking of tomorrow, I think I've found somebody. She's going to come in during the morning to see the place, and I'll get you to show her what's what. I expect your mother would like you to go away as soon as possible, wouldn't she? Where are you thinking of going?'

'Skegness,' I said at random and thought afterwards that it might be a bit too bracing at this time of year, so added 'or Hove' as an afterthought.

The timid creature who arrived the next morning as my possible successor was called Mrs Hopper. She crept about the place with Mrs Vaughan, clearing her throat nervously when addressed, her forehead puckered anxiously under a green cloche hat.

'And now,' said Mrs Vaughan in the hall, 'if you really think you'd like to come to us I'll take you to the kitchen.

Monica can explain things there to you better than I can. I'm afraid I'm no cook.'

I was spared the trouble, however, as they came in together and Mrs Vaughan, having nothing better to do, stayed and conducted the tour of the kitchen herself. I was able to go on peeling potatoes while she rattled off details of our domestic routine. She knew all about cooking and housework in theory, anyway. It was one of the many accomplishments of her extraordinarily versatile brain that she could discourse at length on the principle of any subject under the sun, unhindered by the fact that she would be unable to carry it out in practice. I had heard her telling Mr Vaughan how to play golf when he came home tired and discouraged on a Sunday evening, and really, though perhaps a little tactless, it was very sound text-book advice. She could give instruction, too, on how to drive a car, with illustrations of road signals, though apparently the only time she had ever taken the wheel had been the last day on this earth for two chickens and a baby pig.

When she had finished she left us, and Mrs Hopper, bewildered and docile, accepted her suggestion that she should stay and have a cup of tea with me.

We didn't get on particularly well together, I'm afraid, as I was feeling excited and rather distrait, and she was one of the most painfully self-conscious women who ever crooked a little finger over a kitchen cup. She was desperately anxious to make it clear that she was a cook-general only from necessity and not from station.

'Just a temporary thing this is for me,' she said, nibbling genteelly at a small crumb of bread; 'it's never been my lot to serve, you know.'

I was in no mood to tell her such things as: 'Everyone that humbleth himself shall be exalted', which is what she would have liked to hear, or to paint a rose-tinted picture of domestic service for her encouragement. I sat silent, thinking, and she, though slightly daunted by my churlishness, cleared her throat a bit and tried to keep the conversation going.

'Of course, I wouldn't really be doing this sort of thing at all,' she pursued, 'were it not for certain unhappy circumstances. Poor Mr Hopper was taken from me all too soon; he wasn't able to provide for me as he would have wished.'

I was uncertain whether this meant that one ought to express sympathy for Mr Hopper's demise or for his incarceration, so I let it pass, and his wife became even more convinced of my uncouthness and began to show a desire to leave, but an inability to make the move. I was called away to open the front door to Clare, who had come to lunch to help dispose of last night's chicken, and when I got back to the kitchen I found that Mrs Hopper had hopped it. We hadn't arranged what time she should arrive the next day, so I ran out of the back door in the hope of catching her on the outside staircase. I was just in time to see the top of her hat, like an inverted pudding basin, descending spirally to the street below. I yelled at her with no result, so I gave it up and leant against the railing thinking about life.

Watching the green blob becoming smaller and smaller made me wonder what I should think of my year and a half of servitude when its memories had diminished too. I was still too near to it at the moment to regard it as anything but a most depressing chapter of my life, and I wondered whether I should ever find myself in the position of people who talk about their school days as the happiest days of their life with no idea of being untruthful. They forget the misery that they may have suffered – that agony of spirit that nearly all children and very young people know and no grown-up can understand, because they have already forgotten.

Our memories are merciful; they store up details of happiness much more readily than details of sorrow. We, however, respond ungratefully by indulging our innate passion for self-torture by turning remembrance into regret. In the end the memory of something perfect becomes even sadder than the memory of despair, for we torment ourselves with the thought that it can never be quite the same again.

When the first agony of a real sorrow has faded, though the sorrow may remain, natural resilience makes the mental picture of oneself in the throes of it fade too. Happiness is so easy to picture that one dwells almost morbidly on some lovely memory, harping on the fact that it is gone, exaggerating, imagining, comparing the present unfavourably, until there you are in floods of tears and almost ready for the gas-oven.

'Ah, well,' I said, turning to go in, '*c'est la vie.*'

'Ho, yes, we had one but it died,' said the grocer's boy, rounding the last turn of the staircase and handing me half a pound of prunes and a packet of soap-flakes.

Although I hadn't been at the Vaughans' more than about ten weeks it was long enough to make me quite an institution. They were a very die-hard family, hating change, and when it came to the point they thought they were sorry to see me go, and felt quite tender towards me.

There happened to be a family dinner on that last evening and I was quite drawn into the conversation, almost as if I had been sitting at the table with them instead of running round it with the steak-and-kidney pudding.

It is a curious game that people like to play sometimes, drawing out the maid (baiting the butler in some houses), in order to get amusement out of the screamingly funny idea that she may have some sort of a human life of her own. Nice people like the Vaughans laugh with you, others laugh at you; but it comes to the same thing in the end. Once you get used to the idea of being suddenly hauled out from the oblivion of servitude into the spotlight of attention, and expected to provide entertainment until they just as suddenly tire of you, and intimate that you have said your piece, it's quite an easy game to play. You have to humour them by saying amusing and slightly outrageous things so that they can retail them to their friends, or 'dine out' on quotations from your conversation.

Frances started it this evening. She was feeling arch tonight, which was unusual for her, so she said: 'I believe I know why Monica's leaving; that young man of hers has come up to the scratch at last!'

I smiled politely, waiting to see whether they wanted to play or whether they were going to start talking about something else. I was quite ready to oblige, but I wasn't going to waste any energy. Clare took it up.

'Has he proposed? How thrilling! What did he say and where did he do it?'

This was the cue for me to become side-splittingly unconventional.

'What a thing to say, Miss Clare!' I said, handing her husband the potatoes from the wrong side, 'you know I don't care for men.'

'What about that Adonis I saw you talking to outside the lift the other day?' asked Mr Vaughan with his mouth full of pie.

'Pardon, sir? I didn't quite catch. A – what?'

'Adonis. Good-looking chap, you know. Good God!' (aside to Clare) 'don't they give these girls *any* education?'

'Oh, him,' I said, ignoring this slight on one of the most famous girls' schools in London, 'that was only the lift man in his Sundays. He's no oil-painting.'

The thing was getting a bit laboured. I hoped they'd soon get sick of it, but they were determined to give me a break on my last evening.

Frances again: 'I'm sure I saw you with a red-haired man at the "Odeon" last week. Honestly,' looking round the table, 'I was sitting just behind them. If you're not engaged to him, Monica, you certainly ought to be.'

'Miss Frances! May you be forgiven. My friend's a married man. His wife's away at the moment so I'm simply keeping him warm.' I rounded this off with a daring wink, and felt that I had done enough. I wanted to take away the pie and see whether they had left any kidneys for me.

Mrs Vaughan thought I had gone a bit too far with my last remark and hastily turned the conversation away from me before I could pollute anyone's mind, so I was able to escape gladly to the kitchen. Not one single kidney! Really, I thought, people are gross. Greed is only pardonable in those one loves very dearly or in oneself.

After dinner I was yelled for from the drawing-room to go and say good-bye to the younger members of the family whom I wouldn't see tomorrow. Nurse had drifted away with Peter during the afternoon without so much as a nod to me. To her I was one of those things that one hopes to exterminate by pretending they are not there.

I sidled in, wiping my hands on my apron, and when I saw them all sitting there, the picture of a family happy in the old-fashioned way, that is rare enough nowadays, my heart quite warmed to them and I could almost have wished that I was staying on amid this nice contented atmosphere. Almost, but not quite.

Clare was sitting on her father's knee, busily engaged in pattering the top of his bald head with lipstick. Her husband was dropping pipe-ash over a photograph album that he was looking at with Clare, who was being roared at by her father: 'For God's sake, why can no woman ever look at photographs without putting sticky fingers all over them?' Clare's husband had decided that she was, after all, quite fetching and was absent-mindedly stroking the back of her neck while he noisily appreciated the humour of his father-in-law.

Mrs Vaughan was darning socks. This was a complicated business, as she couldn't darn without her glasses, and for some unknown reason she couldn't talk if she had them on. To darn without talking would have been agony, but on the other hand, in view of the pile of socks in her basket she didn't feel justified in talking without darning. The result was a complicated exercise of taking the glasses off, losing them, finding them, and putting them on, losing her needle, dropping the sock, picking everything up, and just getting ready to attack a hole, and then thinking of something to say and starting the whole thing over again.

'There you are, Monica,' she said, removing the encumbrance once more, 'they just want to say good-bye before you go.'

It had undoubtedly been her suggestion, but they all shook me dutifully by my red and rather sodden hand – I had just been washing up – and wished me luck.

My last morning dawned in a grey drizzle of rain, but nothing could damp my spirits on this auspicious occasion of 'positively my last appearance in this or any other country' as cook-general. I walked through the streets under my father's umbrella, unchastened by the thought of what he would say when he found I had taken it without asking.

An impulsive and short-lived consideration for Mrs Hopper made me have a sketchy round-up of some of the dirt and mess that was my legacy to her. I cooked a large breakfast for Mr Vaughan as a token of my goodwill, and he lingered over it and, rushing off to the office in a hurry, forgot to say good-bye to me. His wife, when she realized this, was across the hall and out of the front door like a bullet. She caught him waiting for the lift, and I heard him complaining slightly, like a small boy who has been told to go and wash his hands. He stumped back to the kitchen and blurted out, 'Good-bye, Monica, it's been so nice having you with us,' at the top of his voice, as if he were addressing a large crowd behind my left shoulder, and hurried away again.

'What, no tip?' I thought as the lift gates rattled and crashed.

Mrs Vaughan made me ashamed of my graspingness by presenting me before I left with a most beautiful pair of bedroom slippers made of white rabbit fur that had been bought for Frances but discovered to be too small.

Mrs Hopper arrived at twelve o'clock, and was established in the kitchen in a black dress and a black full-length apron that sported a great many pink cabbage-roses but no waistline. She had a curious way of accompanying all her actions with a *sotto voce* running commentary of spoken thoughts. I left her making an apple pie, and could hear it going on in the distance while I took leave of my mistress in the hall.

'Three ounces of butter – weigh it out – that's right. Now, let me see, I must have six ounces of flour; here's the bin, it looks as if it could do with a clean. How much sugar? Sugar, sugar, where are you, sugar? This must be it; the supply seems rather low. I'll put it all in. Apples – one, two, three, four, five, six; will that be sufficient, I wonder?' and so on as a background for the kind and solicitous remarks that Mrs Vaughan was pouring into my undeserving ear.

'Now, be sure to come and see us when you're passing and tell us how you're getting on.' (This was probably what Miss Nitchin had been told, too.) 'Take care of yourself. Tell your mother from me that you ought to go on an acid-free diet; do you all the good in the world. I used to say the same thing to Maud, but she never paid any attention.'

'Oh, you will give her my love when she comes back, won't you, madam?'

'Of course. She ought to be back next week. It's wonderful that her mother's so much better. Maud won't have so much to do for her any longer. Well, good-bye, and be sure – Oh dear,' as a crash came from the kitchen followed by a feeble wailing. 'I believe that's Mrs Hopper in trouble already, I'd better go and see. Good-bye again.' She rushed away, so I had to call 'Good-bye, madam,' after her. I knew the timbre of every crash and clatter that could be got out of that kitchen, and this one was only the old familiar story of the oven shelf being pulled out too far and falling to the ground, sometimes accompanied (as in this case) by a pie-dish that had been standing on it.

I shut the front door behind me on poor Mrs Vaughan at the start of a fresh saga of contretemps. The people who deserve perfect service never seem to get it; I suppose because they are too indulgent. It seems hard when one thinks of the cantankerous devils whose staff hop round them with the immaculate efficiency of terror.

It seemed funny to be swanking out of the flats by way of the lift and the main entrance instead of clattering down the iron staircase at the back. It was the epitome of my glorious freedom and as such gave me a terrific thrill.

Returning to the family bosom, I found it heaving sighs of relief at the ending of what they had written off as a period of strange and regrettable madness. I began to realize what they had to put up with from me, in the way of exhausted and moody silences, or occasionally hysterical scenes of rage and tears.

'Oh, well, she can't help it, poor fool, she's tired,' or 'Don't tease Monica, she's not herself tonight,' they said good-naturedly, pitying me in my lunacy. It really was a little hard on them that the only repercussions they felt from my being a cook should have been such unpleasant ones. I determined to be a little ray of sunshine in future, tripping about the house, scattering joy and gladness on all who crossed my path. On this nauseating vision I fell asleep and slept, off and on, for about a week, only waking to open my mouth for food and drink and to scrub myself frenziedly in hot baths. I was haunted by the thought that the smell of the kitchen still hung about me, as if domestic service were loth to let me go from its clutches. At last I began to feel a bit more pure, and I rose from bed and bath a new woman.

I found that quite a lot of money had accumulated in the bank as the result of earning wages that I had had neither the time nor the energy to spend, and in my desire to live in a way as far as possible removed from what I had been through I went out and spent the whole lot in a very short time on the adornment of my person.

I broke out in no uncertain way in a search for the fun that I had missed for so long. With the strident cacophony of gaiety I tried to drown the cold little voice inside me which soon began to mutter disparaging remarks.

'Isn't all this just leading back to the same point of boredom from which you tried to escape before? And when you get there,' it seemed to say, 'then – what?'

© ALAMY

Monica Dickens, 1940